the
star chefs
cookbook

by Richard Bramble

edit... Locke

Published by Blake Publishing Ltd,
3 Bramber Court, 2 Bramber Road,
London W14 9PB, England

First published in paperback in Great Britain 2002

ISBN 1 85782 540 3

British Library Cataloguing-in-Publication Data:
A catalogue record for this book is available from
the British Library.

Designed by Graeme Andrew and Richard Bramble
Editorial Coordinator – Adam Parfitt

Printed and bound in Italy by
Eurolitho S.p.A, Milan

1 3 5 7 9 10 8 6 4 2

BLAKE

302444

contents

addendum to first edition

The very nature of Michelin Star Chefs and their restaurants means that sudden changes are a rarity, never the less progress steadily takes place. Four years have passed since the first edition and I felt it an appropriate time, whilst reprinting, to note these changes within the text. Michelin Stars have been gained and lost, some chefs have new restaurants whilst others have closed, meanwhile the chefs continue to cook. This is a healthy process, which plays its part in the development of cooking and restaurants within the British Isles.

My passion for ingredients, be it painting a herd of Jersey cows, sea trout fishing, diving for scallops or painting wild boar to list a few, has inspired and lead me to create a whole new series of ingredient study paintings and prints. Commissions regularly take me into the secret kitchens of the chefs, each one having its own unique life. Creating the Aubergine design for Gordon Ramsay's dress plate six years ago, inspired a range of limoge porcelain ingredient plates which Jersey Pottery now make.

One of the most inspiring aspects of creating this book was painting in the kitchens, working with the young chefs and seeing them develop. Many now have their own restaurants, and it has been a real pleasure working artistically with them in their new ventures. I can see it will only be a matter of time before a new artistic culinary journey will be needed to celebrate their cooking!

Richard Bramble
London, 2002
www.richardbramble.co.uk

I dedicate this book to the Bramble family. Through your
unconditional love you have shown me the way.

A NOTE ABOUT MEASUREMENTS
Almost without exception, the chefs featured in this book have supplied their
recipes using metric measurements. These have also been listed in imperial, but such a
conversion is of necessity approximate. As the recipes require a certain degree of
accuracy, it is recommended that the metric measurements are used.

Details of all the restaurants featured in the text can be found towards the end of the book

foreword

Some time ago, I gave my permission for a young artist to paint a watercolour of one of my restaurants. I was impressed with the results and Richard soon became a familiar face around the kitchens, his enthusiasm for the food and the surroundings showing itself in his work.

The chef and the artist are involved in much the same process: the creation of something exquisite from the most basic of ingredients. And both processes can become fraught. Chefs, at the best of times, are not the easiest people in the world. Richard's achievement in his art is matched only by his ability to have persuaded so many great talents and grand temperaments to appear in one book. He must, at times, have felt like a lion tamer.

This book is the result of four years' work, and one that Richard should feel as proud to have created as I feel to be a part of.

Marco Pierre White
London

introduction

Some of my earliest memories are of family holidays on the Atlantic coast of the Outer Hebrides. Here I would dive for scallops and catch monkfish in lobster pots, then cook them on the beach to eat in the freshest way possible. On other occasions I would fly-fish for brown trout and, on the way home, stop to pick wild mushrooms. It was no accident that I developed a love of good food and was perhaps inevitable that one day I should want to celebrate fine cooking through my art.

I remember the day I first had the initial idea for such a celebration. It was the winter of 1995 and I was drawn by the vibrancy inside a restaurant I happened to be walking past. It was so full of life, so colourful ... it seemed such an exciting era for chefs. Almost immediately I put on my thermals, set up easel in the street and started painting. I had just started to cook my own dinner parties and a growing interest in food preparation gave me the extra impetus to get to know the chefs personally. My plan at first was for nothing more than to put on a show of the paintings with a catalogue including recipes from the restaurants. As the chefs started to open up to an artist in their midst, I began to think I might be able to create a unique book, a portrait of excellence, told through art and my own special anecdotes. Once for example, Anton Mosimann's food buyer, Willie, suggested that I go to meet their mushroom supplier, Mrs T, in a wood somewhere between London and Bournemouth.

Woods all look the same to me so, not wishing to find myself lost, I arranged to meet her at home. I arrived bright, but not too early, on a Monday morning at nine o'clock. Mrs T opened the door in her dressing gown and had difficulty staring at me through one half-open bleary eye – she had been up until the early hours the night before sorting mushrooms. No doubt, she would have preferred not to have had a smiling stranger on her doorstep but, with admirable politeness, she invited me in for a coffee before we got going. Not much was said as I sat opposite her two solemn Great Danes, though I quickly learned that her best wood was a closely-guarded secret, and she insisted that if she took me there I must keep quiet about it. 'You're never to tell anyone, otherwise I'll take you to an average wood.'

As I followed her deep into a strange, shaded land, the adventure started to feel all a bit 'Brothers Grimm' – had a witch flown out of the dense trees ahead the fairy tale impression would have been complete. Anyway, we found the spot and I worked like crazy for three hours picking mushrooms, carefully cutting them in the appropriate way, depending on the variety, to ensure they would grow back correctly. We then put them into ordinary carrier bags. On our way back, if Mrs T saw anyone coming, I was ordered to hide the bags as best I could. If you have ever tried to pretend to be an idle stroller, whistling with one hand thrown nonchalantly into pocket with three bulging bags of bulbous fungi behind your back, then you know just how absurd this exercise is.

Before I returned to London we went to the local pub for lunch. She pushed me to see if I remembered where the wood was – I said I couldn't. I honestly could not find my way there again without Mrs T. And even if I could, I would not tell – I do not want to live out the rest of my days as a toad. On another occasion, I found myself travelling up to the wilds of Scotland in the hope of meeting the elusive Gunn Eriksen, whose kitchen at the Altnaharrie Inn was steeped in mystique and rumoured to be something of an alchemist's den. Her recipes once got no further

than the ingredients and the food preparation itself, leaving the diner to marvel in ignorance at the mouth-watering dishes. Many never get to see Gunn. I was lucky and managed to sit down with her for five minutes, however, all I got that day was a painting of the outside of the inn.

Such stories need to be written up and fortunately for me, though probably not for him, I have Jake Locke to help me with the writing. Even though Jake joined me relatively close to the end of the project we have shared numerous gastro-adventures, from the hilarious to the embarrassing: I shall not forget in a hurry the time I could not stop giggling every time a

certain French wine waiter starting talking – not recommended in a Michelin-starred restaurant.

As I have already said, my love of food grew from my experience of fresh ingredients, and the best dishes I have eaten are the ones I have caught myself. For me, one of the most pleasurable aspects of working on this book has been my being allowed into the different kitchens, seeing the food being prepared. Sometimes a chef has cooked a dish just for me and helped my understanding by tracing the ingredients back to source. Indeed, it is a welcome trend in modern cuisine that the top restaurants and their diners are becoming

country. I am a firm believer in the holistic approach to food and the community and see the natural beauty in seasonal eating as opposed to an all-year-round homogenisation of products which is never going to provide the best in quality.

Everyone's taste varies to a certain extent and the dishes I have painted for this book have been chosen for their ability to transfer to the artist's palette as well as for their effect on the diner's palate; the recipes should allow any enthusiastic home cook to prepare the dishes in his or her own kitchen. You will find short studies on particular ingredients and wine notes from the sommeliers themselves. The wines chosen are all interesting and most can be found with a little extra effort, although one of the graces of a top restaurant is that it does the exploration for you. Of course, the main thread of this book has been the chefs themselves.

The character of the chef has become something of a social archetype, whether this be the knife-wielding moustachioed madman or the flamboyant media star with a string of groupies and legal battles to his name. As an artist I have been somewhat privileged in the open access I have been given to the chefs' kitchens and, to a large extent, their lives. Sometimes I have been caught between volatile rivalries, hearing stories that would make your toes curl, each individual ego demanding that I remain loyal to him or her. Try telling a modern chef you are neutral – it's a bit like North Africa saying to Rommel and Montgomery in World War II that it will not play host to the fight. The chefs, however, have been courteous to me and more than willing to help with this book; they have made it the celebration it is. I hope you enjoy it as much as I have.

Altnaharrie Inn

increasingly aware of where the food comes from. I have now met many suppliers, from an asparagus farmer whose family has been farming for four hundred years, to a husband and wife who left the world of big finance in the City to build a farm with some of the best naturally-reared rare breed meats in the raymond blanc

When I did my first painting at Le Manoir aux Quat' Saisons, I was sitting outside in the vegetable garden and had fallen asleep in the warm sunshine. I was woken by a big fat rabbit jumping out of a lettuce patch and landing heavily at my feet. When I showed Raymond Blanc the picture, he told me about the fight to clear the garden of ground elder plants and the thousands of rabbits living there. First he tried to reason with them, then ply them with piles of cabbage leaves which they completely ignored – indeed, every method in the book was used in an attempt to decimate the rabbit population. He then surrounded the gardens with fencing buried deep into the ground. I must have been woken up by one of the few survivors! The garden is now thriving and Blanc grows more than 80 varieties of vegetable and herbs organically.

Stories like this add to the unmistakable charm Le Manoir holds for me. Later, when I came to discuss the book more seriously with the chef, the timing could not have been worse – he was up to his eyes in a mammoth restructuring and refurbishment programme. Planning permission had just been turned down by the council, so

it was understandable that his attention was diverted. I remember he was having a management lunch with his head chef and I was sandwiched in between the two trying to strike up a conversation, but getting no more than monosyllabic answers. I decided to finish my food, get out rather quickly and assume Raymond Blanc wanted nothing more to do with the project. The next time we met, the reception was warm and, since then, the influential chef has done all he can to accommodate me at his Oxfordshire restaurant, helping with increasing enthusiasm.

Raymond Blanc was born and raised in the small village of Besançon, in eastern France. Although not interested in cooking at the time, he became aware of the changing seasons and built up a respect for harmony and contrast by enjoying various country pursuits, spending enchanted nights hunting for frogs or lazy afternoons fishing for trout. In most French households life revolves round meal times and the rituals and customs of the table are rarely forgotten. Raymond Blanc still refers to this at the start of his menu:

The table remains a powerful symbol of friendship and celebration of life. In my family we could just about read the menu by listening to the conversation – a light start with drinks, the crossing of the bread by my atheist father followed by the main course of massive discussions on religion, garnished with politics and, of course, the topic of sex for dessert ... at which point my extremely devout Catholic mother would hurriedly leave the room.

At eighteen he left college with no specific

interest, but wanting to do something creative. The story goes that one day he was inspired by seeing the evening terrace of a restaurant surrounded by trees and illuminated by gas lamps. What followed was a round of lowly jobs in local restaurants before he did his military service. Here, not having much to do, he started to think about his professional life and decided to go to England where he could work without a catering education.

In 1972, at the age of twenty-two, he arrived in England and set about learning the language with all the determination of a man possessed; he also learnt German over an eight year period. At first he had to force himself to stay in the country, but gradually it became his home; he found some close friends and he fell in love with England, albeit with caution. 'Twenty years ago it was such a primary country, little sensitivity with lifestyle … the British were so reserved, keeping all these feelings behind. I had two male friends and it took them fifteen years to tell me they each had a mistress … a Frenchman would tell you within five minutes.'

He got a job at The Rose Revived, a restaurant and hotel on the banks of the Thames which allowed him to experiment with a few ideas in the kitchen. He started to become motivated by the progression of a dish, from choosing ingredients through to the final preparation. Blanc read through as many books

Bramble 96

on the art and craft of cooking as he could find, choosing from the start to teach himself rather than work under any one master chef; he believed that what he might lack in guidance he would gain in the freedom to indulge his curiosity. 'Being self-taught you do not carry the baggage of education … you do not have the traditional masters ramming the "Escoffier bible" down your throat.'

In 1974 he married and, though the marriage was eventually to fall apart, it gave him two children, Oliver and Sebastian. In 1975 The Rose Revived head chef walked out taking the entire brigade with him. Blanc took over and,

after two years, the restaurant was rewarded by an entry in Michelin and one AA star. In 1977 he opened Quat' Saisons in Oxford, humbly situated between a lingerie shop and Oxfam. He rocketed to culinary fame in a few years, with Egon Ronay deciding that Raymond Blanc was one of the few chefs who can be truly called an 'artist'. In 1983 he fell in love with Great Milton Manor, originally a prebendal manor dating back to the Norman Conquest, and on which site was eventually built the rambling fifteenth-century Cotswold house, now a Grade II Listed Building. With the help of a few friends he transformed the

property into the magnificent country house hotel and restaurant, Le Manoir aux Quat' Saisons, set in thirty acres and complete with 17th century ponds (the perfect place for romance), formal gardens, geometric vistas, croquet lawns and bronze contemporary statues. Even before it opened in 1984, Blanc had built up such a reputation it was awarded two Michelin stars in advance.

Le Manoir has changed again, but at the heart of it is still the frail-looking Frenchman who oversaw the operation from a temporary portacabin; scattered everywhere were the pages of a draft text for a health book he was helping to write. Raymond Blanc is not old, but he has already had one stroke and the workload, before he even steps foot in the kitchen, is heavier than ever: hotel additions, a new conservatory, guest drawing room and champagne bar. There is a new private dining room with its own kitchen, a new cookery school, kitchen and bakery, nine new bedrooms and a large landscape programme. As Blanc says, 'It is not just the patching of a hole … it is a complete reinvention, a complete renaissance.' He fought for three and a half years for planning permission and, effectively, spent over a million pounds. Because it was delayed, building prices rose. Blanc remained phlegmatic through it all, though stress, undoubtedly, took its toll. With such a huge project he is, however, aiming to set new standards in the industry and wants to create a completely different Le Manoir, where food, welcome, elegance and warmth will be second to none.

The new Le Manoir is about the perfect use of space, in the building and in the cuisine; Raymond Blanc is involved in every part of the project, especially when it comes down to the aesthetic. 'I am a passionate man … my mind does not work any other way. Movement

inspires me to do everything I do. Manoir is to be the first country house to go on a quest for the twenty-first century.'

Indeed, the heart of Le Manoir is the food around which it aims to give the guest a complete experience, and genuine care, something that he thinks restaurants in London rarely offer now because they have become 'cynical'.

When Raymond Blanc first thought about owning a restaurant he just wanted a small place, somewhere he could call 'home sweet home'. He soon discovered that life does not quite follow a fixed plan. 'It's like saying, oh, my girl is going to be tall, brunette, with green eyes … and she's so so pretty, she's like a goddess … she is kind, she is motherly, she is gentle and thoughtful without being oppressive … and then you fall in love with a small blonde with red eyes who gives you hell all your life. That is life … there is so much of life you don't plan … that is its beauty and drama.'

Loyalty is important to Blanc and it is an excellent experience for any young chef to work at Le Manoir. Blanc is proud that his people work *with* him and not for him. To date, thirteen

Michelin guide chefs have worked under Blanc. It is a tough school of thought, but people here have the opportunity to grow and this, perhaps, is the most rewarding side for him. His brigade is loyal and each has a part to play in creating a dish. Blanc works patiently with his largely British staff, eating with them, pushing them, trading knowledge by example, encouraging everyone to deepen his or her understanding. Despite his mission to help others in their development, his own reputation is in no danger of fading into the background. He is regarded as being one of the finest chefs in Europe, creating dishes of brilliance and artistic integrity.

He is the *complete* chef, combining art and science and under-standing many of the myriad elements that have an influence on his cooking, such as soil types, irrigation, weather conditions, indeed the whole process from seed to table. This is why Blanc's cooking reflects the seasons so much more than most. But it has not always been a finely-tuned operation. When he first came to Britain in the '70s, he was disgusted with the quality of the ingredients available, the result of a cycle of standardisation in which the consumer unquestioningly accepted the inferior. He remembers there being a lack of markets in which to buy fresh fruit; fresh fish was virtually 'non-existent'. He is, however, happy that the industry is acquiring a respectable image, though even now it is hard to get the very best. 'We are not interested in the good … we are interested in the sublime – that's the difference.' With its volume of trained people, TV exposure and books, Blanc certainly has an influence.

As yet, Blanc has no plans to take it easy – he is very excited about the future possibilities of a friendly spa and the detoxification centre with its aim to cleanse people with food. Since 1999 a successful cookery school has been running with the students staying at Le Manoir for a number of days. And being in partnership with Richard Branson, there will be no shortfall in marketing strength. Like the Virgin boss, Blanc is an ideas man. That is why Le Manoir is so unique.

One new side of the business is the successful brasserie chain, Le Petit Blanc, offering the best food at affordable prices in a 'fun' atmosphere. They stick to a traditional French country base, but the chefs are allowed to add their own creativity to the menu. So far there are brasseries in Oxford, Cheltenham, Manchester and Birmingham. Each is different, the design built around the original architecture.

Le Manoir itself will continue to provide some of the best cuisine in the UK, intelligent and honest, and Raymond Blanc will continue to move with the times. Ironically, Blanc has little time for the one thing that first inspired him, the ritual of the family meal. He does occasionally find the time to go fishing, but is aware that it 'takes a whole day'. He likes to walk, to sketch, to read as often as possible. He likes poetry and Dostoyevski. 'Dostoyevski is the greatest writer I have read. I particularly like what he did with *The Idiot*. His study of people is unbelievable – the way he can break up the soul and the mind into millions of pieces.' Raymond Blanc's own study is that of food, in which there is no lack in curiosity and intensity.

truffle macaroni with langoustine tails

ingredients

12 langoustine tails

4 baby artichokes

1 courgette

1 baby leek

200 g (7 oz) baby spinach

20 macaroni pieces of 8 cm length

12 truffle slices

For the Langoustine Jus

400 ml (13 fl oz) olive oil

600 g (1 lb 5 oz) onions, finely chopped

200 g (7 oz) celery stalk, finely chopped

400 g (14 oz) fennel trimmings

4 cloves of garlic, skin on, crushed

6 sprigs of thyme

rind of 2 oranges, dried

40 g (1½ oz) tomato purée

1 kg (2 lb 3 oz) tomatoes, chopped

1 kg (2 lb 3 oz) langoustine carcasses, intestine removed

100 ml (6 fl oz) cognac

SERVES 4

First make the langoustine jus. In a large, heavy based pan, heat 200 ml (6 fl oz) of olive oil and add the onions, celery, fennel, garlic, thyme, orange rind and tomato purée. Sweat for 30 minutes on a low heat, not allowing the ingredients to colour. Then add the chopped tomatoes and cook for a further 15 minutes.

Next, in a small pan, reduce the white wine to about half its original volume. Then, in a separate pan, heat the remaining olive oil. Finely chop the langoustine carcasses and sear in the olive oil for two minutes. Add the cognac and cook for 10 seconds, then add the reduced white wine and the tomato and vegetable mixture. Barely cover with cold water and simmer for 15 minutes. Add the chopped chervil and tarragon, cook for a further 2 minutes and pass through a chinois. Set aside.

Now prepare the truffle cream. In separate pans, reduce the cream by about a half, the port by about two thirds and the madeira by about two thirds. Warm the stock gently, then place all the liquids together in a blender and blitz for 2 minutes. Then dice the butter and add that, along with the truffle trimmings and blitz for a further 1 minute. Pour into a bowl and season. Set aside.

Next, peel the baby artichokes into 400 ml (13 fl oz) water with the juice of 1 lemon, then cook gently in olive oil for 10 minutes or until tender. Slice the baby leek into 5 cm batons, cook in boiling, salted water until tender and then refresh in iced water. Cut the courgette into 5 mm slices.

800 ml (27 fl oz) dry white wine

4 sprigs of chervil

8 sprigs of tarragon

For the Truffle Cream

250 ml (8 fl oz) double cream

100 ml (3 fl oz) white port

100 ml (3 fl oz) madeira

100 ml (3 fl oz) white stock

10 g (½ oz) truffle trimmings

100 g (3½ oz) unsalted butter

Place the macaronis into a large pan of boiling water and cook for 4 minutes. Meanwhile, pan fry the baby spinach, cut the artichokes into quarters and in separate pans heat the artichoke quarters and cook the courgette slices, then set aside.

Next, quickly pan fry the langoustine tails and keep warm. Warm the sauces and adjust seasoning to taste. Thoroughly drain the macaronis and then roll them through the truffle cream. Divide between four bowls, arrange the spinach, courgette, leek and artichokes around and place the langoustines on top. Pour the langoustine jus over the langoustines and garnish with the truffle slices.

 Il Vignola VDT Avignones, Tuscany Sauvignon Blanc 1996

'Foeniculum dulce'

Fennel is grown for its seeds, leaves and for its swollen edible bulb known as Florentine fennel, which all have a mild aniseed like taste. Usually biennial, forming a bulb or thick root the first year and flowering the following summer. It will last for years and grows best near the sea on chalky inland soil. The leafs are fine and soft, the flowers yellow. Divided into two sub species although not very distinctive. 'Vulgare' is the wild sweet tasting fennel – both seeds and leaves have a centuries old reputation of being an excellent herb for flavouring fish with. 'Azoricum' and 'Dulce' form swollen bulbs, the edible part being the leaf bases. The bulb has to be harvested very early in its growth, stems no more than a foot high, for the bulb is in fact the expanding leaf stalks and any more growth and there will be no bulb to speak of.

As a herb it was cultivated in the early Assyrian and Babylonian gardens. It is native to the mediterranean shores and was taken to Northern Europe and Britain by the Romans. It later was one of the nine sacred herbs of the Anglo-Saxons, who used it in cooking and as medicine. The Florentine fennel was introduced into England in the 19th century from Italy where it is eaten cooked or raw, traditionally accompanying cheese and fruit for dessert.

seabass with langoustine and herb butter

ingredients

65 g (2 oz) sauce vierge

18 g (½ oz) red wine sauce

1 x 220g (8 oz) jumbo langoustine

15 g (½ oz) herb butter

1 x 120g (4 oz) seabass fillet

1 tsp dried thyme and orange powder

280 g (10 oz) sun-dried cherry tomatoese

50g (1¾ oz) artichoke and tomato mix

For the Artichoke and Tomato Mix

400 g (14 oz) baby artichokes

300 g (10½ oz) large fennel

300 ml (½ pt) olive oil

20 g (½ oz) sugar

15 g (¾ oz) salt

a little pepper

a squeeze of lemon juice

SERVES 1

First prepare the artichoke and tomato mix. Peel and julienne the fennel then blanch with 100 ml (3 fl oz) of the olive oil, some pepper, salt and lemon juice. In another pan, quickly fry the baby artichokes in the remaining oil with the rest of the ingredients, including some salt, pepper and lemon juice. Mix both together.

Next, season the seabass with the thyme and orange and pan fry, skin side down, for 5 minutes. Turn over and cook for a further 1 minute. Quickly pan fry the langoustine. Re-heat the sauce vierge and arrange around a plate. Spoon together the artichokes, fennel and tomatoes in the centre of the plate and arrange the seabass on top. Cut the langoustine in half, and place the pieces around the edge of the plate. Finish with thin streaks of the red wine sauce.

 Château de Selle Rosé 1996

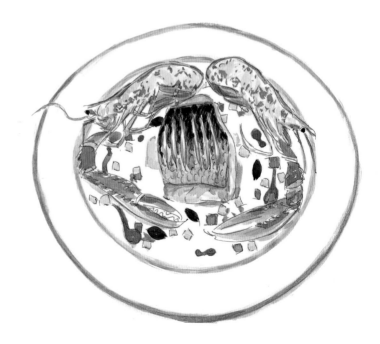

millefeuille of red mullet

ingredients

145 g (5 oz) squid buttons

200 ml (7 fl oz) extra virgin olive oil

50 g (1¾ oz) sun-dried tomatoes

32 g (1 oz) fresh croutons

a few sprigs parsley and coriander, chopped

8 x 50 g (1¾ oz) fillets red mullet

8 large scallops

65 g (2¼ oz) spinach and rocket

a few parmesan shavings

For the Squid Ink Risotto

a little butter

12 g (½ oz) shallots, finely diced

60 g (2 oz) risotto rice

60 ml (2 fl oz) white wine

salt and cayenne pepper

1 tsp squid ink

180 ml (6 fl oz) fish stock

1 bay leaf

½ star anise

½ liquorice stick

a little thyme

½ clove garlic

SERVES 4

First make the risotto. Reduce all the ingredients except for the butter, shallots and rice to about 120 ml (4 fl oz). Sweat the shallots in the butter for three minutes, then add the rice and cook gently for another 5 minutes. Add the two mixtures together, cover, and cook very slowly until the rice is tender. You could add a little parmesan and cream before serving.

Now, fry the scallops in a hot pan for about a minute until they colour. In a separate pan, fry the squid, and then add the tomatoes, herbs, grated parmesan and croutons. Quickly fry the red mullet in a non-stick pan, flesh side first and then finish with the skin side. Wilt the spinach and the rocket in the hot olive oil.

To serve, place some risotto on the bottom of an oval plate, and spoon on the squid mix. Put two red mullet fillets together so that they form a whole fish, and place this on top. At each end of the plate put 1 scallop (this could be placed on some fennel purée, if desired). Garnish the plate with some spinach layered with parmesan shavings. This dish is good served with a saffron sauce.

 Mersault les 'Meix Chavaux' 1994

palette of sorbets

For the Palette

125 g (5 oz) flour

125 g (5 oz) butter

125 g (5 oz) icing sugar

200 g (7 oz) egg whites

For the Caramel Ice Cream

1 lt (1 pt 13 fl oz) milk

250 g (9 oz) caster sugar

40 g (1½ oz) glucose syrup

15 g (½ oz) butter

80 g (2¾ oz) water

200 g (7 oz) egg yolks

200 g (7 oz) whipping cream

SERVES 8

First make the ice cream. Heat the milk in a pan. Put 200 g (7 oz) of the sugar with the glucose syrup into a separate saucepan and cook until you have a dark caramel. Add the butter and water, and stir until smooth. Gradually add the hot milk, then the egg yolk, remaining sugar and whipping cream. Cook up to 85°C, and then cool on a cold bain-marie. Churn in an ice cream machine.

To make the palettes, soften the butter and mix it with the icing sugar. Sieve the flour and fold it slowly into the mixture. Shape into 8 palettes on a baking tray and cook in a medium oven at 190°C/375°F/Gas Mark 5 until golden. Leave to cool.

Serve the palette with a selection of ice creams and sorbets, such as the caramel ice cream, fig ice cream, pistachio ice cream, cinnamon ice cream, mango sorbet, raspberry sorbet and blackcurrant sorbet.

 Muscat de Lunel 'Clos Bellevue' 1996

cassoulette nougatine

ingredients

For the Nougatine

750 g (1 lb 11 oz) caster sugar

375 g (13 oz) glucose

340 g (12 oz) flaked almonds, roasted

For the Amaretto Filling

50 g (1¾ oz) vanilla crème anglaise

15 g (½ oz) Amaretto

75 g (2½ oz) whipped cream

For the Poached Apricots

100 g (3½ oz) water

330 g (11½ oz) caster sugar

55 g (2 oz) lemon juice

a little extra water

12 apricots

60 g (2 oz) Archers liqueur

For the Floating Island

200 g (7 oz) egg whites

250 g (9 oz) caster sugar

½ vanilla pod, grated

milk for cooking

SERVES 6

First make the poached apricots. Cut each apricot into 4. Heat the water and caster sugar until you have a light caramel. Add the lemon juice and a little water to stop it cooking. Bring to the boil again and add the apricot quarters. Simmer for about 2 minutes, and then add the Archers. Pour into a tray and cool in the fridge.

Now make the floating islands. Place the egg whites, sugar and vanilla in a mixer and whip until firm. Use a large spoon to shape them into large quenelles and cook them in hot (not boiling) milk for about 10 minutes. Leave to cool.

For the Amaretto filling, simply whip the cream with the Amaretto and add this to the crème anglaise.

To cook the nougatine, bring the sugar and glucose to a blond caramel. Add the almonds, and place the mixture on Teflon trays to cool down. Break into blocks, and then crush to a fine powder. Sieve the crushed nougatine about 1 mm thick onto a silicon mat, then cook in the oven at 170°C/350°G/Gas Mark 3 for about 7 minutes. Use a circular cutter, 12 cm in diameter to make 6 bases. Use a 9 cm cutter to make 7 lids. Heat each base individually over a flame, and then shape them with a bowl. Heat the lids and shape them with a big ladle. To serve, put the base on a plate and put 2 poached apricots inside. Top with the floating island, and then cover with the Amaretto filling and the nougatine lid. Pour the apricot cooking juice around.

Jurançon Clos Uroulat 1991

anton mosimann

When I had the initial idea for this book my immediate challenge was how I was going to meet some of the most renowned chefs in Europe: I mean, I wasn't the most well-connected artist in London's culinary circles. I thought the best way to do this was if I just started painting in front of their restaurants – as most of my paintings take a few weeks to finish I was bound to bump into the chefs sooner or later. Mosimann's private dining club is a converted Presbyterian church in London's Belgravia and, with its 19th century Gothic façade has, from an artistic point of view, always been a favourite of mine. Not surprising, then, that the paintings of Mosimann's were the first I did. I remember taking my easel across to West Halkin Street on the hunch that even this most private of personalities would be too curious to avoid me for long.

The first time I saw Anton Mosimann he made an immediate impression when he pulled up early one morning in his sleek black Jaguar car, not unlike an important overseas dignitary arriving for a state function.

Fashion might dictate changing taste, but style never passes the sell-by date and there is no substitute for experience and quality. Mosimann is like a rock. Born in Switzerland in 1947, he is a fourth generation chef whose parents ran a restaurant in the small town of Solothurn. Very early in life, he acquired his acute business acumen and, more importantly,

realised 'how much pleasure a good meal can give'. It is this that set him on a path to learn as much as he could about cuisine from every part of the world. It began with his being awarded the Diplôme de Cuisinier at the tender age of seventeen, then rapidly accelerated with his driving his first sports cars – to become a life-long passion – across the Alps to work in Rome and the rest of Europe, then Canada, Japan and Scandinavia, before arriving at The Dorchester in 1975. A year later he became the youngest ever maitre chef de cuisine when he was only twenty-nine. Through it all he was fuelled by an ambition to transfer all his knowledge in creating his own environment that would give both him and his customers immense enjoyment. At The Dorchester he set about refining the traditional haute cuisine to create a lighter, more natural version. Mosimann invented Menu Surprise: six feather-light courses created using only the freshest ingredients straight from the market that day, where the guest would not know what he was going to eat until it appeared at his table. As an artist, I believe the way you are as a person is reflected in your work: Anton Mosimann's innovation, his care and attention to detail, pervades all his work and is the reason why the other top chefs hold him in such high regard.

As hoped, Mosimann and I did finally meet and, although the exchange of words was

minimal, I got the chance to explain my idea for this book to him. Without hesitation he offered to do all he could to help and agreed to my coming inside to work on a painting of his kitchen. It was the first kitchen I had painted, and what a kitchen. The first difference I noticed is that Mosimann employs rather more women than average in what remains a male-dominated profession. The chefs still wear the traditional tall white hats. During the busiest restaurant times, when orders are flying in thick and fast, an onlooker might be forgiven for thinking that a performance is underway, a kind of opera in which at any moment it would not be out of place for a lead soprano to appear from behind the pots and pans and launch into a dramatic aria. My own experience was further enhanced by my setting up my painting gear in

Mosimann's office, in front of a large plate glass window overlooking the kitchen. I learned later that this 'window seat' is a popular position with some diners to come and eat and watch the 'performance' at the same time.

Before I could start work on the kitchen picture I was whisked up to the eaves of the old church to a bar that hangs above the dining room. Mosimann and most of his staff were there, cracking open bottles of champagne as a goodwill gesture for a member of staff who was leaving. I had been asked to share a glass or two and was made to feel at ease as Mosimann wished the leaver all the best for the future. I also got to know the pastry chef quite well. I must say, from an artist's point of view, if I were a chef I would choose to work in the pastry section. Here, raw ingredients are transformed, as if by magic, into

meal rather well. I'll never forget hearing Mosimann's voice coming towards the kitchen as the pastry cook handed me his creation. Not wishing to compromise my resident artist position at the club I swiftly whipped the incriminating article behind my back. Simultaneously, Mosimann swung round the corner and greeted me with his usual smile, then looked to my fresh painting: 'Waiting for it to dry, Richard?' To this day I am not sure whether he meant the art or the tart.

Having spent many weeks painting in the club, I noticed that Mosimann never raises his voice, and he is always considerate and patient with his staff. In turn the staff always appear welcoming and willing to learn, and Mosimann seems to gain much satisfaction in seeing his kitchen run in a happy atmosphere. The old maxim, you get as good as you give, is certainly apropos at Mosimann's.

Perhaps kindness is nothing unusual in a man who has been trained in the traditional way from the age of sixteen. Family values instilled in him at home have remained important to this day. In his book, *The Essential Mosimann*, he talks about eating at home:

Our home was the restaurant ... I grew used to the fact that we were rarely alone as a family, even at Christmas when my father would invite those without families of their own to share our food ... I think it made me more aware very early in life how much pleasure a good meal can give.

He is sensitive to people and understands that staff need to feel valued and part of a team. Chefs often start their careers as teenagers working in strange kitchens far away from home, often in another country. It is not

exciting new creations. With meat, fish and vegetables, it is often the case that the less you do the better. Anyway, I asked Mosimann's pastry chef if I could work on a painting of a lemon tart; as the item was off the menu at the time he had to make a whole tart just for me. By pure coincidence I happened to have a dinner party that evening and subtly hinted that I might take the tart along as it would round off the surprising that the kitchen, staff and head chefs become their new home and family while they search for the support and leadership they need to learn and grow. Therefore, a good chef will lead by example. I spoke with a chef who was once at the bottom of the rung working as a *plongeur* (washer-upper) at The Dorchester. He remembers Mosimann always knowing everybody's name and birthday, and making sure they were celebrated – and this was with a staff of a hundred and fifty!

First and foremost, Mosimann is a professional, and his love for the profession can be witnessed at The Mosimann Academy, established in 1995 in Battersea, London. Here he teaches and, being an avid collector, has over 6,000 old cookbooks. One of the oldest, and certainly the finest, was written in 1605 by Bartolomeo Scappi, master chef to Pope Pius the Fifth. Mosimann has written a number of books of his own, including *Cuisine Naturelle*, *Mosimann's Fish Cuisine* and *Mosimann's World*.

canapés with sushi

MAKES ABOUT 30 PIECES

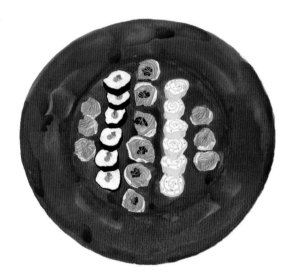

ingredients

12 ml (½ fl oz) Japanese rice vinegar

30 g (1 oz) caster sugar

450 g (1 lb) short-grain rice

100 g (3½ oz) each of three kinds of seafood, filleted

1 tsp wasabi (green horseradish)

several sheets nori (dried layer seaweed)

strips of cucumber, peeled and de-seeded

strips of green and red pepper

sesame seeds

250 ml (8 fl oz) dark soy sauce

25 ml (1 fl oz) mirin (sweetened rice wine)

handful of fresh chives, finely chopped

For the sushi rice dressing, mix together the vinegar and sugar, add salt to taste and leave overnight to steep. Wash the rice well under some cold water for 5 minutes and leave to drain for at least 30 minutes. Place in a heavy-bottomed pan and add 850 ml (1 pt 8 fl oz) cold water. Bring slowly to the boil. Increase the heat to high, cover and boil for 3 minutes. Reduce the heat to low, and cook for 5 minutes. Now pour the sushi dressing over the rice and mix. Fan the rice to cool it rapidly to body temperature, mound in a bowl and cover with a damp cloth.

Cut the fish, some into small chunks, some into slices. Spread a little wasabi on some of the seafood and press a block of rice on the top. Other pieces of fish can be rolled in chives or sesame seeds.

For an ideal canapé, wrap some fish, pepper slices, cucumber and rice in strips of nori. To make a sauce for this, heat the soy sauce with the mirin in a small pan for 2-3 minutes, then cool.

 Blanc de Blancs Billecart-Salmon Vintage Champagne

zucchini and saffron risotto

ingredients

25 g (¾ oz) butter

1 small onion, finely chopped

200 g (7 oz) arborio rice

a good pinch of saffron threads

1 litre (1 pt 13 fl oz) hot chicken or vegetable stock

250 g (8¾ oz) small courgettes, trimmed and blanched

50 ml (1¾ fl oz) dry white wine

a little extra butter

freshly grated parmesan cheese

2 tbsp chives, finely cut

salt and pepper

SERVES 4

Halve the courgettes lengthways, scrape out the middles and slice into crescents. Melt the butter in a pan, add the onion and cook gently for 2-3 minutes. Add the rice, stirring to coat it thoroughly with butter. Add the saffron and about 150 ml (5 fl oz) of the hot stock and begin to stir. Over a medium heat, keep simmering as the rice absorbs the stock, adding more as required to retain a creamy consistency.

When the rice is almost ready (it should be soft on the outside but with an inner firmness), add the courgettes. A few seconds before you judge the rice to be ready add the dry white wine, which will stop it cooking. Remove from the heat.

Stir in a knob of butter, season and add some parmesan to taste. Sprinkle with chives and serve with a separate bowl of parmesan.

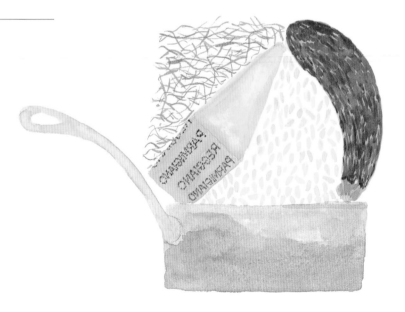

steamed panaché of seafood with cardamom sauce

ingredients

90 g (3 oz) scallop meat

75 g (2½ oz) sole fillets

50 g (1¾ oz) red mullet fillet

210 ml (7 fl oz) fish stock

90 ml (3 fl oz) white wine

60 g (2 oz) white onion, diced

60 g (2 oz) whole carrot

30 g (1 oz) carrot, cut into ribbons

20 g (¾ oz) coriander roots

7 cardamom pods

1 bay leaf

30 g (1 oz) leeks, white parts only cut into ribbons

30 g (1 oz) yellow courgettes, cut into ribbons

a little fresh coriander

15 g (½ oz) tomato concasse

knob of butter

fresh sprigs of chervil or basil

SERVE 4

Mix the fish stock and the wine, bring to the boil and add the onion, whole carrot, coriander roots, 4 of the cardamon pods and the bay leaf. Turn down to a simmer, and then lightly steam each type of fish in rotation over it. It is important that the fish should be slightly undercooked.

In boiling water blanch the leek, courgette and carrot ribbons. Drain and cool. Add the remaining cardamon pods to the warm fish sauce and bring to the boil. Turn down to simmering point, remove the pods and add the coriander and tomato concasse. Heat the butter in a heavy-bottomed pan and add the vegetable ribbons. Once hot, remove and drain.

To serve, place the vegetable ribbons in the centre of a large soup plate, and arrange the warm fish around them. Bring the sauce to serving temperature and spoon lightly over the fish. Garnish with sprigs of fresh chervil or basil.

 Robert Mondavi 1994 Chardonnay

loin of lamb with a mustard and herb crust

ingredients

4 x 150 g (5 oz) noisettes of Welsh lamb

1 sprig thyme

1 sprig rosemary

3 tbsp olive oil, with salt and pepper

2 tsp dijon mustard

3 tsp grain mustard

4 tbsp chives, finely chopped

200 ml (7 fl oz) brown lamb stock, reduced by half

300 g (10 oz) mixed vegetables, peeled and sliced

Trim the lamb well, cutting off all the fat, before marinating in a dish with the thyme and rosemary in the olive oil for at least 2 hours. Wipe off any excess oil from the lamb and season with salt and pepper. Grill for 2-3 minutes on both sides, leaving the centre pink.

Mix together 2 tsp of dijon and 2 tsp of grain mustard together and brush over one side of each piece of lamb. Place the chopped herbs on a plate and dip the mustard-coated side of the lamb noisettes in them, shaking of the surplus herbs.

Heat 1 tsp grain mustard together with the brown lamb stock for the sauce. Stir-fry the vegetables in the olive oil for a few minutes. Season well and divide them between the centre of the four plates. Spoon over a little of the sauce and serve the lamb on top (having finished the lamb in the oven if necessary).

 1986 Château Duhart-Milon-Rothschild

fishcakes with parsley sauce

225 g (8 oz) white fish fillet

225 g (8 oz) salmon fillet

2 tbsp fresh parsley, finely chopped

1 tbsp fresh chives, finely chopped

250 g (9 oz) potatoes

olive oil

butter

salt and pepper

For the White Wine Sauce

400 ml (13 fl oz) fish stock

100 ml (3 fl oz) dry white wine

50 ml (1½ fl oz) Noilly Prat

1 small shallot, finely diced

150 ml (5 fl oz) double cream

2-3 tbsp fresh parsley, finely chopped

salt and pepper

SERVES 4

First make the white wine sauce by combining everything but the cream and the seasoning in a saucepan and reducing by half by fast boiling. Add the cream and gently simmer to reduce the sauce to a coating consistency. Remove the pan from the heat and strain the sauce through a fine sieve. At this stage, set aside 2 tbsp of the sauce for the fishcakes. Mix the fresh parsley into the rest and liquidise until smooth. When ready to serve, reheat gently and season to taste.

Now cut the salmon fillet into ½ cm cubes and mix and bind with the parsley, chives and white wine sauce that you have reserved. Season to taste with salt and pepper. Boil the potatoes for 5 minutes in salted water. Cool, peel and grate them, squeezing slightly to get rid of any excess moisture. Place on a plate and season well.

Shape the fish mixture into eight balls. Roll these in the grated potato to coat the fish all over, then flatten into fishcake shapes. Heat a little butter and olive oil together in a non-stick frying pan and sauté the fishcakes on both sides until crisp and golden brown. Drain well on kitchen paper. Serve with the parsley sauce poured around.

 Sauvignon-Blanc Baron de L. (de Ladoncette)

bread and butter pudding

30 g (1 oz) butter

3 small white bread rolls

250 ml (8 fl oz) milk

250 ml (8 fl oz) double cream

a pinch of salt

1 vanilla pod, split

3 eggs

125 g (4½ oz) sugar

10 g (¼ oz) sultanas, soaked

20 g (¾ oz) apricot jam, sieved

icing sugar to dust

SERVES 4

Preheat the oven to 160°C/325°F/Gas Mark 3. Cut the bread into slices, lightly butter a large ovenproof dish and use the rest of the butter to spread over the bread slices. Arrange the bread slices in the base of the dish.

Place the milk, cream, salt and split vanilla pod in a pan and gently bring to the boil. Mix the eggs together until pale then gradually add the milk and cream mixture to the eggs, stirring well to amalgamate. Strain into a clean pan.

Add the milk and the sultanas to the bread in the dish. The bread will float to the top. Place the prepared dish in a bain-marie on top of folded newspaper and pour enough hot water to come halfway up the sides of the dish. Bake in the preheated oven for 45 to 50 minutes. When the pudding is ready, it should wobble very slightly in the middle. Remove from the oven and cool a little.

To serve, gently heat the apricot jam, thinning with a little water if necessary. Lightly brush a thin coat of the warm glaze over the top of the pudding, then dust with icing sugar. Serve slightly warm.

 Veuve Clicquot White Label Demi Sec Champagne

symphony of fruit purées

ingredients

250 g (9 oz) apples, peeled, cored and sliced

200 g (7 oz) blackcurrants, stemmed

1 large mango, peeled and stoned

1 paw-paw, peeled and sliced

200 g (7 oz) kiwi fruit

200 g (7 oz) raspberries

4 tsp natural yoghurt

juice of 1 lemon

a little caster sugar

a little apple juice

a few wild strawberies or raspberries

a few tiny sprigs of mint

SERVES 4

Cook the apples until soft in a minimum amount of water with a little lemon juice and sugar. Allow to cool, and then strain through a fine sieve. Thin with a little apple juice if necessary and then chill.

Bring the blackcurrants to boil in a little water with a little lemon juice and sugar. Once cool, purée and strain through a fine sieve. Thin with a little mineral water if necessary and chill.

In a liquidiser, separately purée the mango, paw paw, kiwi fruits and raspberries, straining and thinning down with a little mineral water if necessary and chill.

To serve, place a scoop of each cold purée onto four large plates, arranging them around the plate. Place a teaspoon of yoghurt on top of each scoop of blackcurrant and raspberry purée. Keeping at plate level, tap it firmly on a solid surface covered with a cloth to spread the sauces out. Take a cocktail stick and draw a continuous spiral several times around the purées, starting from the yoghurt. Garnish with wild strawberries or raspberries.

Robert Mondavi, Chardonnay, Napa Valley California – This compares with the best. Only the Gallo brothers have rivalled Mondavi as a force in California's winemaking. The winery combines state of the art equipment and a personal knowledge of every French barrel maker worth a hoot! A winning combination creating top quality wine on an industrial scale. The sweetness of the scallop and the variety of the fish, combined with the richness of the creamy cardamon sauce make chardonnay the best match.

Billecart-Salmon Blanc de Blancs Vintage Champagne – From the house founded by Nicolas-François Billecart and still in the family, blended from all the Grand Crus from the Côte des Blancs giving it surprising length. Ideal for an aperitif with its complex aroma of white flowers with a subtle addition of soft red fruit. Perfect with these sushi canapés.

Château Duhart-Milon Rothschild 1986 Bordeaux Medoc – This rich, powerful claret coming from a tongue of land north of Bordeaux town called medoc would suit the lamb. This type of wine peaks between the ten and fifteen years old mark. It comes from a vineyard that was bought by the Rothschilds in 1964, being right next door to their château Lafite, and has since been completely replanted and enlarged. As the young vines come of age this is becoming a great château again.

Pouilly-Fumé Baron de L – Baron Patrick Ladoucette's vineyards export half the production of this exclusively to restaurants. Made from the Sauvignon blanc grape it has a green freshness, and is powerful and aromatic matching the fish cakes well.

michael caines

When I first visited Gidleigh Park, I was greeted with the sound of the North Teign River running its virile course through the garden just fifty yards in front of the house. An amicable stranger ambled past and looked up from under a floppy hat: 'You'll find brown trout in there, and sea trout and salmon.'

When the sweet wood smoke reached me at the front door I already had an appetite. I passed a neat row of communal pairs of green wellies, and the odd brightly-coloured croquet ball to enter the wood-panelled hall. I noticed the old grandfather clock, its hands telling the wrong time, as if time were not that important. Staring at me was Brown, the Havana Siamese cat. And then Michael appeared, fast on his clogged feet.

Michael Caines is one of only a handful of chefs to have been awarded a Michelin star before the age of thirty. After graduating as 'top student' from Exeter College, he found his mentor in Raymond Blanc, working at Le Manoir aux Quat' Saisons for three years. Taking 'RB's' advice, he went to France to 'finish' his skills, doing a year with Bernard Loiseau at La Côte d'Or in Saulieu, Burgundy, followed by another in Joël Robuchon's 'SAS of kitchens' in Paris. In 1994 he returned to England to take on the challenge of lead role in the restaurant at Gidleigh Park, a country house hotel in the middle of Dartmoor, owned by Paul and Kay Henderson, a charmingly eccentric couple. Since then, Caines has been awarded five red rosettes by the AA, an accolade made to chefs at the top of their profession and, in 1996, his dishes attracted the vote for Restaurant of the Year in *Decanter* magazine. He has achieved this despite a car accident in which he lost his right arm three months after succeeding Shaun Hill as head chef at Gidleigh.

Michael Caines is not shy of his skills. A natural confidence paired with his rising success makes him quite aware of his market value. 'Every chef I've worked with has told me I would be successful,' he said calmly, leaning on the arm of his chair.

I asked him if he has always been confident. He put his hand to his chest as part of an immediate answer: 'It's in here.' But he thought about it further, tracing the steps back. He would not say he had a tough childhood, but he was the black adopted son brought into a large family in Exeter, an area with minimal first-hand experience of so-called ethnic minorities. His parents instilled solid values in him and this helped him to remain calm when the more ignorant members of the community tried to express themselves with racial abuse. The affronts taught him to dig deeper within himself, to carve out his own integrity and identity, which would still be standing when the mindless were starting to wonder why their own lives had not amounted to much.

At home he learned to cook because it was 'better than washing up', though he soon came to enjoy it. He cannot remember any early burning desire to be a chef. In fact, he was not sure what he wanted to do when he was about to leave school; he had always been active, so joining the Army was one possibility. In the end, through not having a better idea, he followed a friend who had already decided to go to Exeter College. 'It was there something clicked,' Michael recounted with a smile, 'and I knew I wanted to devote my life to cooking. It was a realisation, the first time in my life I'd had a sense of what an "opportunity" meant.'

After leaving college he first worked at Ninety Park Lane, then met the man whose flair and originality were to guide him. 'Raymond Blanc influenced me not just in cooking, but in how to be a chef.'

This was an important distinction which helped Michael to make the transition when Blanc thought, in order to evolve, he should go to France to work under the regime of Joël Robuchon, thought by many to be France's greatest chef. 'He is hard-driving,' Michael remembered, 'and my time in his kitchen was the toughest year of my life. But I learned a lot. I developed a respect for flavour, and found out that fine food does not have to be over elaborate.

Three-star cooking isn't any harder than two-star, but it's more consistent, simpler, more pure ... certainly the closest you'll get to the true flavour of the ingredients.'

Relevance is Michael's guiding principle: taste always before presentation. He constantly re-examines his creation, looking for ways to have the same effect with less effort. For him it is nothing more than complete dedication to the flavours, to the effect on the diner's palate. For this reason he will never disguise his food. He believes that the job of the chef is to bring out the natural flavours of each ingredient, to unlock its secrets and give the diner an honest

experience. Every time he constructs a dish, he builds up a mental catalogue of flavours and combinations – this is his value to the kitchen, to the restaurant. For this reason he uses local suppliers and gets to know the whole operation, for example how a lamb has been reared, the history of the land on which the organic beef has been raised, who caught the fish, or precisely when the fresh herbs were planted. It was he who bullied the gardener into planting a wider variety of herbs and baby vegetables.

But the local method is not without its problems. 'Being out of the way, we get two deliveries a week ... if nothing goes wrong,' Michael pointed out. 'Joël got two deliveries a day in Paris ...'

The extra effort, however, is worth it as you can really taste something of Dartmoor when dining at Gidleigh.

Michael likes nothing better than to wind down the evening with a glass of champagne, and when I was there he invited me to join him. I asked him how he deals with the growing media attention and the competitive circus which is the inner circle of the most well-known names in British cuisine. 'I prefer to keep one step away from the press.' He paused to pour out another glass of champagne. 'Why compete?' He said emphatically, 'Success will come naturally to any man who has talent, who believes in himself and who is prepared to put in

the work and the hours. Learn your trade. Don't ever rush things. A star chef must continue his success if he is to be a *great* chef. You must stand the test of time. Learn your trade first, age is not important, some people take longer to mature, like a fine vintage wine.'

Michael Caines believes in things happening in their own time, when conditions are right. 'Do you believe in luck?' I asked.

Michael looked me straight in the eye. 'The more I practise, the luckier I get.' He smiled. 'Gary Player used to say that, when people said how lucky his golf shots were. No, I don't believe in luck.'

Indeed in 2000, his practise was acknowledged with two Michelin Stars.

'I'm completely at home at Gidleigh Park,' he continues 'it's the perfect platform on which to build my craft. I grew up in Exeter, so working here keeps me close to some old friends, and I can swim in the river after hot lunch services.'

In 2000, 'Michael Caines at the Royal Clarence' was opened, with a bar and a cafe attached. This brought his elemental style to the centre of Exeter and new life to this established hotel, which is located opposite the beautiful Cathedral.

He is, however, aware that people change and grow, that as well as evolving as a chef he is evolving as a person. 'A successful man will naturally come into contact with the finer things of life.' He looked thoughtful: 'Modern cooking is the perfect arena for transcending class, race, education ... anything that keeps people apart.'

a tian of marinated aubergine, peppers and tomato with roasted scallops

ingredients

10 large scallops, cut in half

olive oil to serve

greek yoghurt to serve

caviar to serve

For the Marinated Aubergines

4 large aubergines

300 ml (½ pt) olive oil

100 ml (3½ fl oz) balsamic vinegar

1 clove garlic, sliced

5 sprigs thyme

4 basil leaves, bruised

salt and pepper

For the Tomato Concasse and Tomato Oil

200 ml (6 fl oz) olive oil

5 basil leaves, finely chopped

1 tsp chopped thyme

8 plum tomatoes, blanched, halved and de-seeded

25 g (1 oz) balsamic vinegar

salt and pepper

SERVES 8

For this recipe you will need 4 small moulds, 55 mm in diameter, and a 55 mm circular cutter.

First prepare the marinated aubergines. Cut each aubergine in half and then cut out the flesh, leaving each aubergine about 15 mm thick. Mix 200 ml (6½ fl oz) of the olive oil with the balsamic vinegar, garlic, thyme and basil. In an ovenproof frying pan heat the remaining olive oil. Season the aubergines and then seal for 15 seconds skin side down. Flip and then cover with aluminium foil. Place in a hot oven for 5 minutes until they are soft in texture. Place the hot aubergines into the marinade, and leave for 4 hours.

Now prepare the tomatoes. In a flat, small roasting tray heat 100 ml (3½ oz) of the olive oil, add the tomatoes and season with salt, pepper and chopped thyme. Place in a hot oven for 4 minutes. Once soft, remove from the oven and add the balsamic vinegar, remaining olive oil and chopped basil. Place into a bowl and leave to marinate for 4 hours. Remove the tomatoes and chop into a small concasse. Separate the tomato oil from the marinade and put to one side.

Next, roast the peppers. Line a small deep roasting tray with foil. Put the olive oil and peppers in it. Season and cover the peppers with foil, and place in a preheated oven at 170°C/325°F/Gas Mark 3. Cook for 20 minutes, turning every 5 minutes. Remove them from the oven and cool. Peel and remove the seeds. Cut out as many circles as you can for the tian: you will need two of each. Set aside for use later.

To make the tian, cover each end of the mould with cling film, then place a piece of aubergine skin side down in the mould. Season. Then cover it with a circle of red pepper, then a circle of yellow. Add some tomato, then yellow pepper, then red. Season and finally add the aubergine. Place

For the Roasted Peppers

3 large red peppers

3 large yellow peppers

200 ml (6 fl oz) olive oil

salt and pepper

For the Tapenade Vinaigrette

75 g (2½ oz) black olives

1 small clove garlic

1 anchovy fillet

20 g (¾ oz) olive oil

For the Tomato Vinaigrette

6 plum tomatoes

20 g (¾ oz) tomato concentrate

50 g (1¾ oz) olive oil

a few drops of Xeres vingar

salt and pepper

For the Basil Oil

200 g (7 oz) olive oil

20 g (¾ oz) basil leaves

on a tray, then cover with another tray. Place a heavy weight on top of this and leave for 6 hours.

To make the tapenade vinaigrette, place the olives, anchovy fillet, olive oil and peeled garlic in a small blender. Add a few drops of water and blend to fine purée. Remove from the blender and put to one side.

Next make the tomato vinaigrette. Cut the tomatoes in half and remove the seeds. Place in a blender with olive oil and blend to a fine coulis. Pass through a fine sieve and whisk in the tomato concentrate. Season with salt and pepper. Add a few drops of vinegar to taste.

Finally, make the basil oil by heating the oil and basil to 80°C. Then blend for 2 minutes. Pass through a piece of muslin and put to one side.

To serve, take each vinaigrette and dribble five lines evenly across the plate. Dribble the oils over the plate. Then place the tian in the middle of the plate with the mould still on. Put the olive oil into a frying pan. Heat and add the tomato concasse. Season and add some of the chopped basil. Drain off the excess olive oil in a sieve and place five piles of tomato around each plate. Season one side of the scallops with salt and pepper. Using a hot frying pan, fry the scallops in olive oil on one side until golden brown. Place on a plate covered with absorbent kitchen paper. Put onto the serving plate and season with lemon juice. Then pipe a small amount of greek yoghurt on top of each one. Top with the caviar and place each one on top of a heap of tomato concasse. Remove the tian from the mould and serve.

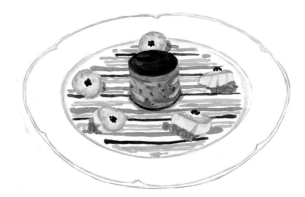

 Vintage Tunina 1995, Jermann

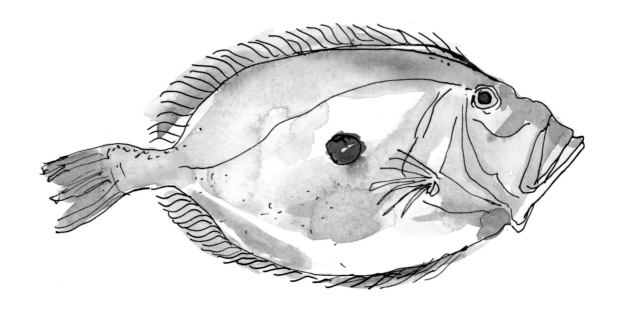

'Zeus faber'

John Dory is found at moderate depths of under 100 metres, mainly to the south and west of Britain. It is most commonly caught by trawlers working over sandy ground. It grows to half a metre in length, is very narrow and has a very large mouth giving the fish a somewhat miserable expression. The jaws hinge forward very quickly into a protrusible tube which is very adept at catching its prey of small fish by sucking them in. The John Dory appears to be a solitary fish with feeble swimming powers mainly using its pectoral fins. Perhaps this is why one can swim up to it in the water, maybe it is a curious fish or lonely. It is good tasting and unusually you can cut three fillets out of each side of the fish. In France it is used in their bouilla baisse and is called Saint Pierre after St Peter. The large black spot on the body has given rise to the legend that St Peter picked up the fish out of the sea of Galilee between thumb and forefinger, leaving two marks. Originally in Britain, the fish bore the plain name 'dory' for 300 years before the addition of 'John'. Perhaps the formation is a humorous allusion to a popular song printed in 1609 about the career of John Dory, a captain of a French privateer.

john dory with a galette of aubergine, tomato and courgette

SERVES 4

First remove the fish's head and cut off the tail. Remove the bony ridge around the edge of the carcass by cutting just inside it. Be very careful not to cut into the flesh. You should be able to make two portions from each fish. Cut the fish in two with a large sharp knife and remove the skin and any untidy bones with scissors.

To make the galettes, first skin the tomatoes and slice into pieces 5 mm thick. Place on a tray, dribble with olive oil, season with salt and pepper and chopped lemon thyme. Place in a hot oven for 3 minutes, remove and leave to cool. Slice the aubergine to the same thickness. You will need 12 slices in total. Slice the courgettes at an angle. These pieces should be the same size as the aubergine pieces. Cook the aubergines in a frying pan with olive oil and salt and pepper until they are brown on both sides. Remove and place on absorbent paper. Cook the courgettes in the same way. Make little piles of the vegetables using 3 pieces of each. Then sprinkle with thyme and reserve for use later.

Next make the sauce. Chop the turkey meat into large pieces. Place a roasting tray with the oil into a hot oven and heat. Add the turkey pieces and roast until they are golden brown. Remove from the oven, and add the onion and lightly colour, then add the garlic head and half the lemon thyme. Roast for 1 minute. Add the water, bring to the boil, and skim. Transfer to a saucepan and simmer gently for 1 hour. Pass through a fine sieve and reduce to 300 ml (½ pt). Then take 20 g (¾ oz) unsalted butter. Place in a saucepan and burn lightly. Add the remaining lemon thyme and some turkey stock. Season with salt, pepper and a dash of lemon and reserve for later.

Now make the breadcrumb mixture. Blend the crumbs finely in a blender. Blend in the parsley and garlic, then pour in the olive oil. Season and pass through a medium size sieve.

For the Provençal Breadcrumbs

300 g (10½ oz) dried breadcrumbs

200 g (7 oz) fresh parsley

50 g (2 oz) olive oil

1 clove of garlic, peeled

salt and pepper

For the Deep Fried Herbs

200 g (7 oz) fresh parsley

100 g (3½ oz) basil leaves

100 g (3½ oz) tarragon leaves

100 g (3½ oz) sage leaves

Next prepare the deep fried herbs. Heat some vegetable oil to 140°C/275°F in a deep sided pan. Add the herbs a little at a time, and cover the pan for safety. When all the moisture is gone from the herbs, remove them from the oil. Place on absorbent paper, sprinkle with salt and keep warm for later use.

You are now ready to cook the fish. Season it with salt, pepper and chopped thyme. Using a non-stick ovenproof pan, heat a little olive oil until almost smoking. Add the fish and place in an oven preheated to 200°C/400°F/Gas Mark 6. Cook for 4 minutes, then turn and cook for a further 4 minutes. Remove from the oven and squeeze lemon juice over the fish. Top with provençal breadcrumbs and grill until golden brown. In the meantime, reheat the vegetables.

To serve, place the fish and the galettes on a plate and garnish with the herbs. Serve the sauce separately in a sauce boat.

 Clos Sainte Hune 1981, Riesling, F. E. Trimbach

passion fruit mousse with pineapple, mango and paw paw

SERVES 8

ingredients

For the Rice Pudding Ice Cream

100 g (3½ oz) pudding rice

100 g (3½ oz) caster sugar

1 vanilla pod

25 g (¾ oz) dessicated coconut

500 ml (17 fl oz) milk

For the rice pudding, blanch the rice for 2-3 minutes and refresh in running cold water. In the saucepan with the rice, add the sugar, vanilla and coconut and bring to the boil. Cook for 30 minutes, simmering gently. Stir occasionally to reduce the cooking liquid. Once cooked, leave to drain in a colander.

To make the clotted cream curd, cream together the eggs, egg yolks and sugar. Bring the milk to the boil, and pour into the creamed eggs and sugar. Put the ingredients back into the saucepan and cook well. Place the clotted cream in a blender and add it to the curd. Blend until smooth. Then place in a bowl and allow to cool.

For the Clotted Cream Curd

95 g (3 oz) milk

50 g (1¾ oz) sugar

2 whole eggs

3 egg yolks

100 g (3½ oz) clotted cream

40 g (1½ oz) Malibu

For the Passion Fruit Mousse

190 g (6¾ oz) passion fruit pulp

190 g (6¾ oz) whipped cream

190 g (6¾ oz) meringue

2 gelatine leaves

For the Fruit Salad of Pineapple, Mango and Paw Paw

passion fruit stock syrup

1 small pineapple peeled and diced

1 mango peeled and diced

1 paw paw, peeled and diced

For the Passion Fruit Stock Syrup

500 ml (17 fl oz) water

150 g (5 oz) caster sugar

1 tsp white peppercorns

8 passion fruit

1 vanilla pod

To serve

a piping bag of melted chocolate

To make the rice pudding ice cream, combine the clotted cream curd, cooked rice and malibu in an ice cream machine. Do not do this until just before serving, as the rice itself should not be frozen.

Make the meringue just before you make the mousse. To make the mousse, soak the gelatine leaves in cold water to soften. Take a little passion fruit pulp and heat. Dissolve the gelatine into this, then add the rest of the pulp and mix well. Cool over ice, stirring occasionally. Add the meringue to the warm fruit pulp and mix well. Carefully fold in the cream. Pipe the mixture into individual moulds, smooth the tops and leave to set in the fridge.

To make the salad, put the water, peppercorns and caster sugar into a stainless steel saucepan for the passion fruit stock syrup. Halve the passion fruit and scoop the flesh into a saucepan. Cut the vanilla pod in half lengthways, and scrape the seeds into the pan, along with the pod. Bring to the boil, then leave to stand for 15 minutes. Pass through a sieve and place back in the saucepan. Take the diced pineapple and add to the stock syrup. Bring to the boil and cook for 10 minutes, then remove from the heat and allow to cool. Once cool, add the paw paw and mango and leave to marinate for 6 hours.

To make the fruit sauce, take 500 ml (17 fl oz) of the stock syrup and reduce to 200 ml (7 fl oz). Allow to cool.

To serve, fill the piping bag with melted chocolate. Pipe a small wedge shape at the bottom of each plate, and carefully fill it in with fruit sauce. Drain the fruit from the stock syrup. Take a 60 mm ring mould, and place it above and to the right of the piped wedge. Fill it ⅓ full of fruit salad, then press it down with a spoon and remove the mould. Heat the mould around the passion fruit mousse, and remove it. Place it on the plate using a palette knife, to the right of the fruit. Put a large spoon of ice cream on top of the fruit salad. Dust the pudding with icing sugar. Serve.

 Tokaji Aszu 1990

pistachio parfait in a tuille parcel

ingredients

6 egg yolks

74 g (2½ oz) sugar

30 g (1 oz) water

75 g (2½ oz) green pistachio paste

250 g (8¾ oz) whipping cream

juice of ½ lemon

For the Tuille Crosses

150 g (5½ oz) unsalted butter

200 g (7 oz) icing sugar

170 g (6 oz) flour

120 g (4 oz) egg whites

SERVES 8

To make the pistachio parfait, cook the sugar and water to 120°C. Beat the egg yolks and, still beating, gradually pour on the sugar and water. Beat until cold. Add the pistachio paste and mix in well on the machine. Whip the cream, and then fold it into the egg mixture by hand. Add the lemon juice. Pour into a deep tray approximately 180 mm x 125 mm. Place in the freezer. Once frozen, use a 55 mm diameter square cutter to cut out the parfaits. Put back on a tray and place back in the freezer.

For the tuille mix, use a mixer to cream the butter and icing sugar until white. Gradually add the egg whites, being careful not to split the mix. Sieve the flour into the mix, being careful not to over-mix. Place in the fridge for 1 hour. Use a spatula to make some crosses on a baking tray. These should be 165 mm in width and 220 mm in length. The middle of the cross should be 55 mm in diameter. Bake in the oven at 160°C/325°F/Gas Mark 3. Remove and leave to cool.

To serve, take a cross, place in an oven at 200°C/400°F/Gas Mark 6 so that it becomes pliable (this should take about a minute), remove from the oven and place a parfait in the middle. Wrap the tuille around the parfait to form a parcel effect and cut off any excess. Serve with a hot chocolate fondant and a pistachio sauce.

jean-christophe novelli

Jean-Christophe Novelli heads the new breed of 'brand name' chefs, personalities whose reach stretches far beyond the kitchen out along the commercial lines of marketing strategy. Novelli attracts notice because of his exciting cuisine and because he is, perhaps, the most obviously handsome of the Michelin-starred men. He swears by his PR guru and she, in turn, must feel a little fortunate in having this user-friendly chef on her books. When I first met him he was already a media star, his face frequently appearing in the press and on TV, targeted at the massive market of potential female fans aged twenty-one right through to sixty-five. Not bad for a small-town boy from provincial Arras in France, a young dreamer who, a few years ago, was plotting his empire between bouts of unemployment and picking strawberries. The success suits his hyperactive mind and means he is rarely in the kitchen any more – he becomes restless easily.

The life of the entrepreneur takes its toll in many different ways: Novelli's frantic appointments schedule is a case in point. One night I waited four hours on the chance that he might arrive and we could discuss his cooking. I was generously looked after by the house and when Novelli did finally make his appearance he apologised profusely and disarmed me completely. 'So, you want to talk about my cooking ... being a cook is the only job where you use all five senses ... like making love.' He looked at me. 'You like a beautiful woman, Richard?'

What could I say? Novelli continued, 'I think I have more passion than most people ... in cooking I develop something which is a five sense mix ... it's all of me.'

Jean-Christophe is keen to simplify things, to reduce them to the essential basics, to get rid of all that is unnecessary. 'When I started cooking there was nothing else ... it gave me cash in hand, food to eat. When I came to the UK I discovered Michelin ... I like the idea of going for something ... I don't like wasting my time.'

'Did you always see yourself as a chef?'

Novelli smiled, pulled out a cigar, almost threw it to his mouth and clenched it between two rows of white teeth. 'What do you think was the first thing I showed my fiancée when I took her to Arras?'

I had no idea.

'I showed her the football ground ... I could have played in the World Cup four years ago.' I smiled.

'You don't know ... you don't know, Richard ... four years ago I was on the dole picking strawberries. If I met you then and I tell you I have a chain of restaurants, you say no way, John. It's all about passion.'

This passion might be the secret of his looking so young despite an average of four hours sleep a night. 'It is the spirit ... it doesn't affect me ... you know, I have not eaten all day, and I'm not hungry. When I go home I relax, then I eat. Before the interview for *Hello!* I went to bed at six in the morning ... I was up at eight. I do not worry about health ... you might have a Bupa, a pension ... you might be dead tomorrow ... I'm not afraid of death ... I have been shot at twice ... I was lucky ... I believe in a spirit ... I believe you are either meant to survive or not, succeed or not, as simple as that.'

As well as fate, Jean-Christophe talks a lot about vision, seeing a person's limitations set by what they believe about themselves. He thinks if you believe in yourself you can overcome the knocks of life. 'If you get hit, it is not the physical thing, it is the pride that gets hurt. Getting hurt is not important ... regret ... the things you didn't do ... that's the worst thing. My only regret is that I didn't play football professionally. It's all about passion ... we are just expositions.'

As well as continually referring to football, Jean-Christophe eats and breathes philosophy: he is a popular philosopher, not unlike Eric Cantona, always ready with a turn of phrase which, if not immediately accessible, does at least sound profound in a way only the French can. He has a theory that the theme of the human being is stupidity in which we expend most of our energy worrying about the second-hand

information other people have given us rather than seeing for ourselves. He thinks humans can suffer the same problems as computers in receiving bad programming in formative years. His aim for himself now, in his own words, is 'to clear up as much shit as possible.'

All this contemplation provides balance to the weight of Novelli's Midas touch, as if the Frenchman has been given the power to turn things to gold but is not prepared to accept this at face value. He started life in an ordinary way with small adventures in his home town of Arras before Military Service in 1979. When I first asked him about this he was quick to make a joke.

'I hear you jumped out of planes?'

'No, I jumped out of submarines.'

He smiled at me and went on to tell me that he has never been so scared in his life. He had never seen an aeroplane before and, for a long time, did not know what they were planning to do with it. He was based in the Pyrenees and built up his strength by doing 70 press-ups a day.

Apparently, he has continued to do this ever since as well as run and go to the gym. He believes that, if you are used to suffering, you build up a resistance and your constitution gets stronger.

When he left the Army he decided to come to Britain because he could not succeed in France, having not gone to catering college and with no diploma to show prospective employers. Rick Stein gave him his first real break in 1990, asking him to work at his seafood restaurant in Cornwall. After a few months, Stein recommended Novelli to Keith Floyd at the Maltster's Arms in South Devon. During this time Marco Pierre White offered Novelli a very good position as sous chef, but Novelli was not yet ready for the pressure of a top London restaurant and chose to stay in Devon. He soon gained his first Michelin star at Provence in Hampshire and finally arrived in

London in a high-profile move to the Four Seasons Hotel in 1993. Although never having worked in one of White's kitchens, Jean-Christophe says that his greatest advice has come from Marco on cooking, technique, philosophy and psychology. It was Marco who was the inspiration behind one of Novelli's signature dishes, Jack in the Box, showing him how to make a pyramid using surfaces of crunchy caramel. Novelli developed this into a caramel box, filling it with chocolate marquise topped with caramel-dipped hazelnuts. All puddings are important to Novelli because they are the last memory the diner takes away with him and image is never far from the chef's mind. The trademark that is completely Jean-Christophe's own is the caramel 'spring', a golden coil which decorates his desserts and features on all his logos. The idea came about by accident after he left a spoon in a pan and returned to find the caramel had wound itself round the metal. After many failed attempts to recreate it he eventually found the solution in a cylindrical knife-sharpener, the steel just cold enough to set the caramel immediately. He once told me that the kitchen always makes a few extra coils to keep in the pastry hatch so that customers can see them as they walk past.

It was Marco's influence that persuaded Novelli to take the plunge and set up his own restaurant in 1996. At the time he had £500 in his pocket, only four full-time staff and, after declining Marco's offer of help, no financial back up. Maison Novelli opened in Clerkenwell Green, EC1, and got its first Michelin star within three months. Novelli remembers the day it looked as if it was all going to go belly-up. 'I sat outside at one of my tables and saw an advertisement for immediate loans. The man was tough, but I borrowed £10,000 … I had no fear that I wouldn't be able to pay him back.'

He did pay him back, quickly, and there was no stopping him. Novelli W8, originally The Ark, opened in Notting Hill in 1997 and started attracting superstar regulars. A two hundred-seat brasserie, Novelli EC1, was opened next to Maison Novelli at the end of 1997 and this was followed by the acquisition of Les Saveurs de Jean-Christophe Novelli W1 in Mayfair to which the Michelin star was transferred. Coincidentally, I first painted this restaurant in 1995 before Jean-Christophe owned it. When I showed it to him he wanted to buy it immediately, on one condition: that I put his name on the canopy.

Novelli is a man who understands the market and he cooks for the public. He claims to be more frightened than most people when it comes to getting the formula wrong. He is shrewd in spreading his risk over numerous ventures so, if one fails, his name stays afloat – Maison Novelli is, without doubt, the heart of the Novelli machine.

Jean-Christophe's ambition is boundless, in 1998 he published his first book *Novelli: Your Place or Mine?* A book about cooking at home with style. I asked him when he thought he would have enough, when he might relax. 'I am not egotistic, I do not do things for ego … I do them because I know I can do them. Chefs get a response immediately for what they do.' He picked up one of my sketches of his restaurant. 'An artist might not gain the respect until after he is dead … then people say, ah, he was good. Then they see the value.'

As if silence was inappropriate right then, he kept the momentum up. 'I am a moron … I drive like a maniac, I lose numbers … the world does not go quick enough for me. I am always before … I am always touching something else … today is today and I forget tomorrow.'

'Is cooking a thing of the past for you?'

'I think I was lucky … I invested in being a chef … I did not know. I could have sold cars, or umbrellas, something, you know … I always spot a chance. Who knows where I will be in ten years' time?'

'Where does this drive come from?'

'It is the vision … success is a state of mind … success mean nothing … success is just a flash … you only say you are successful at the end of the day … then you look back and say, yeah, I done well … success is a non-stop possible, which gets bigger and bigger and bigger … not only on the financial side, but in spirit … it is as important.'

At this point a smoke alarm went off in the kitchen which Jean-Christophe found very amusing. 'Ah, smoked salmon … we are having smoked salmon. The fire alarm always go off when we have smoked salmon.'

Our drinks arrived. On cue, the alarm stopped. 'I don't know where I stop. I am becoming more and more informed all the time. You don't own anything in life, what you have is status ... in terms of a brand name, or a marque, like a statue ... what you leave behind. How many people make millions and nobody knows ... they get crushed in a plane ... who cares? Van Gogh was not successful ... he was eating bread and water, but when he was dead ... Look at Rachmaninov ... why were they successful? Because they left something behind.'

He took a sip of Pernod. 'All is strategy. Why do other chefs continue to work in the kitchen for so long? How long does it take a chef to realise this, that he doesn't have to stay in one kitchen ... it's not just the dishes, it is the strategy. I might get crushed in the Eurotunnel, but my business carries on without me ... I am just a front. The most important thing in any company is the staff, and their trust and loyalty ... you do not need to work eighteen hours a day to achieve this ... you need a leader, someone who helps people to express themselves ... the pleasure for me is to see younger people take over and their desire to succeed. People believe in a leader, that's why it works. My plans are strategic, but I need the support of a good team.'

In business he thinks it important when starting to be accessible, to offer your services as often as possible, for nothing if needs be, to get your name about, to test the market response to your work, to gauge your market worth. Over-stretching his restaurant business, combined with the economic climate has meant in the last few years he has not been so fortunate and has been forced to consolidate with one restaurant, Maison Novelli, and work with business partners. This restaurant is now part of the White Star Line group of restaurants, set up by his friend Marco Pierre white and Novelli is concentrating on consultancy work. I am sure it will only be a matter of time before the ambition and drive of Novelli means that he will embark on a new venture. Novelli is a man who loves to talk the night away, not just working out his own plans, but helping others to realise theirs – he is genuinely happy when things go well for people. When I first told him about this book he looked at me as an older brother might and started to ask questions in an attempt to make sure everything was working for the best. He even offered the services of his PR agent for which he would foot the bill, a testimony to his generosity of spirit.

bay leaf brochette of lamb, shitake, confit of onions and masala sauce

ingredients

1 x 680 g (24 oz) lamb fillet

1 bunch basil leaves

12 shitake mushrooms confit

12 onion confit

4 sticks of long bay leaf branch

½ aubergine

8 baby fennel

6 baby carrots

12 baby leeks

For the Masala Sauce

1 onion

2 cloves garlic

2 tomatoes

25 g (¾ oz) butter

120 ml (4 fl oz) cream

lamb trimmings

25 g (¾ oz) curry powder

1 tsp each of coriander seeds, cayenne pepper, cumin powder, turmeric

4 cardamom seeds

fresh coriander, chopped

SERVES 4

First make the masala sauce by placing the onion, garlic, tomatoes, lamb trimmings, butter and two cups of water together in a pan with half the curry powder and the spices and cook gently for 45 minutes. Add the remaining curry powder and cook for a further hour. Add the cream and then blend in a food processor. Pass through a sieve. Add the fresh coriander.

Now, cut the lamb into 12 equal pieces. Skewer the lamb, the shitake, the aubergine and the onion confit onto the bay leaf branch. Repeat, finishing off each kebab with a piece of lamb. Cook all the remaining vegetables in boiling water until soft but still slightly crisp. Meanwhile, pan fry the kebabs on all sides until nearly cooked. Finish them off in an oven at 250°C/475°F/Gas Mark 9.

To serve, heat the vegetables in the sauce and serve with a brochette and a sprig of chervil to garnish. This can also be served on a bed of cous-cous.

 Santa Carolina Merlot Reservado 1997 Chilean

tartare of marinated trout

100 g (4 oz) fresh salmon trout

100 g (4 oz) sea salt

500 ml (17 fl oz) olive oil flavoured with herbs and garlic

2 sticks asparagus, cooked

¼ cucumber, sliced

1 tsp caviar

1 quail egg, cooked for 2 minutes

salt and pepper

For the Tomato Dressing

10 ml (¼ fl oz) tomato juice

200 ml (7 fl oz) olive oil

10 ml (¼ fl oz) white wine vinegar

1 tsp icing sugar

For the Anchovy Mayonnaise

1 egg yolk

1 clove garlic

1 tsp basil and parsley

4 anchovies

1 tbsp sherry vinegar

1 tsp Pommery mustard

250 ml (8 fl oz) olive oil

SERVES I

Marinate the salmon trout in the sea salt for I hour. Wash, and then marinate in the olive oil for 24 hours.

Make the tomato dressing by blending the tomato juice, icing sugar and vinegar and then slowly adding the olive oil, blending all the time. Then make the anchovy mayonnaise, by mixing all the ingredients except the olive oil in a blender. Then slowly add the olive oil, blending constantly.

Dice the salmon trout and the asparagus into ½ cm cubes and mix together. Mix in I tbsp of the mayonnaise and then place the mixture in a pastry ring. Layer the sliced cucumber on the top, remove the pastry ring and transfer the trout tartare to a plate. Place the quail egg on top of the cucumber with a little caviar (at the base and top of the egg) and add a few chive sprigs. Pour the tomato dressing around the outside and serve.

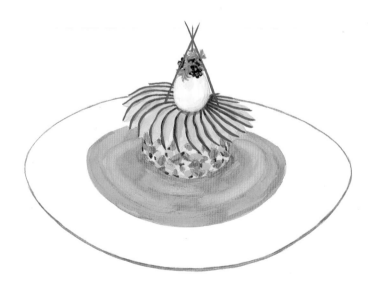

 Quincy Pierre Duret 1996

'Abramis brama'

Sea Bream come from the enormous sparidae family of fishes which is mainly tropical and subtropical. They are mostly stockily looking with Roman noses, and a large spikey dorsal fin. They generally grow to a few pounds in weight. They are found on rough rocky bottoms swimming in shoals feeding on shellfish. Hence their grinding teeth. In the U.S.A they call them 'Porgy' and they are popular in Japan often eaten raw.

Red bream is the commonest member of the family "Pagellus bogaraveo" is found in the British channel and Ireland in fairly deep water. Annually they move up the west coast and into the North sea. Seconded to the Gilt-head for taste. A large black spot at the beginning of the lateral line. Black banded bream are the second most commonest bream found in British waters. 'Spondyliosoma cantharus' found around the south and west coast annually migrating to the eastern end of the English channel where considerable numbers congregate. Its common name is 'old wife'. The Gilt-head bream is the best tasting of the group. 'Sparus aurata' is rare in British waters, the name comes from the golden band between the eyes.

gilt-head seabream on coriander risotto

ingredients

4 fillets fresh sea bream, with the skin scored

250 g (9 oz) cooked risotto base

50 g (1¾ oz) coriander

1 tbsp fresh parmesan

1 tbsp mascarpone

For the Lime Oil

1 lime, chopped

1 tbsp icing sugar

75 ml (2½ fl oz) olive oil

For the Chilli Caramel

2 red chillies, de-seeded, finely chopped and blanched

2 tbsp white wine vinegar

1 tbsp caster sugar

1 tbsp water

1 drop olive oil

SERVES 4

First make the chilli caramel by sweating the chillies in the oil and then adding the sugar, vinegar and water. Cook until it turns to a syrup.

To make the lime oil, blanch the chopped lime in boiling water for 30 seconds and then refresh. Place the lime in a blender with the icing sugar and olive oil. Process and strain the oil off, and set aside.

Now make a coriander purée by liquidising the coriander in a blender with 2 tbsp water. Melt the marscapone in a pan and add the risotto, parmesan and coriander purée. Heat through and season to taste.

Place the sea bream skin side down in hot oil. Cook until the skin is crisp and the fish is almost cooked through, then turn just before serving with the risotto, lime oil and chilli caramel.

 Santa Carolina Sauvignon Blanc Reservado 1997 Chilean

roast seabass, chorizo, confit aubergine infused with picholine olives and sun-dried tomato juice

SERVES 4

ingredients

4 x 185 g (6 oz) seabass fillet

8 baby fennel

40 g (1½ oz) picholine olives, stoned and halved

6 cherry tomatoes

10 slices chorizo sausage

6 pieces aubergine confit

1 litre sun-dried tomato juice

2 bay leaves

1 sprig rosemary

3 sprigs chervil

10 leaves basil, shredded

1 clove garlic, chopped

olive oil

salt and pepper

For the Sun-Dried Tomato Juice

1 box tomatoes, sliced

4 red peppers, sliced

3 heads of garlic, peeled and sliced

First make the sun-dried tomato juice. Place all the ingredients into a large pan and mix well. Cover very well with cling film, bring to the boil, and then leave above the stove (but not on the heat) for 24-48 hours. When this has been done, pass the mixture very slowly through a muslin. Pour into a pan, reduce to a caramel, and then whisk in the butter.

Next, make the aubergine confit by slicing the aubergine into rounds and placing it in a roasting tray with all the herbs and oil. Place in the oven at 180°C/360°F/Gas Mark 4-5 for 30-35 minutes. Remove, and allow to cool in the roasting tray.

Now, pan-fry the seabass on both sides with the bay leaves. Place the fish in an oven pre-heated to 220°C/425°F/Gas Mark 7 for 5 minutes or until the skin is golden brown and the fish is just cooked. Warm the baby fennel in some boiling water. Then heat a little olive oil in a frying

100 g (3½ oz) basil

50 g (2 oz) rosemary

500 g (1 lb) sun-dried tomatoes

200 ml (7 fl oz) white wine

200 g (8 oz) shallots, peeled and sliced

3 onions, peeled and sliced

10 g (¼ oz) unsalted butter

salt and pepper

For the Aubergine Confit

1 aubergine

500 ml (1 pt) extra virgin olive oil

pan and add the fennel, chorizo sausage and olives. Season well and then cook lightly. Add a quarter of the tomato juice, the garlic and the basil, and heat. Arrange the mixture in the centre of the plate with the aubergine confit. Place the seabass on top. Pour the remaining tomato sauce around the plate, garnish with sprigs of chervil, and serve.

 Brouilly Domaine Des Esnards 1996

1 bay leaf

1 piece rosemary

4 shallots

1 clove garlic, crushed

salt and pepper

boîte surprise

ingredients

4 squares of light sponge, dimensions 2½ in x 2½ in x ½ in (6cm x 6 cm x 1.3 cm)

a little brandy

For the Chocolate Mousse

113 g (4 oz) extra bitter chocolate

1 tsp brandy

5 egg whites

60g (2 oz) caster sugar

SERVES 4

First, grease 4 individual moulds (2½ in x 2½ in x 2½ in). Brush the sponge squares with brandy and place one in the bottom of each greased mould. Now make the chocolate mousse. Start by melting the chocolate with the brandy. Then, whisk the egg whites to soft peaks and fold in the sugar. Fold the chocolate into the egg mixture, and then fold in the whipped cream. Fill each mould with the mousse, and leave to set in the fridge for 1 hour.

To make the nougatine boxes, first cook the sugar with the liquid glucose in a heavy pan until you get a golden caramel. Remove from the heat, pour onto lightly-oiled greaseproof paper and cool. When brittle, break the caramel up and place two-thirds in a blender with the coconut or ground almonds. Process to fine grains, like caster sugar.

300 ml (½ pt) double cream, lightly whipped

For the Nougatine

550 g (1 lb 3 oz) caster sugar

2 tbsp liquid glucose

4 tbsp desiccated coconut or ground almonds

For the Decoration

90 g (3 oz) peeled hazelnuts, lightly roasted

8 small strawberries

3 tbsp icing sugar

Now, on a non-stick baking sheet, sprinkle the powdered caramel in a very thin and even layer, the dimensions of which should not be less than 12 in x 12 in. Heat the tray in a hot oven (220°C/425°F/Gas Mark 7) or under a grill until the caramel has melted again and formed a thin glassy layer. Leave to cool, but before the caramel has quite cooled, and using a ruler and a very sharp knife, score it into neat squares. You will need 24 squares: six per box. When quite cold, break off and separate the squares.

Now remove the mousses from the moulds and stick a square of caramel to each side and to the base, leaving the top open. Cut the remaining squares in half and, using some of the remaining caramel heated as glue, stick them to the top, open like lids.

To decorate, dip the hazelnuts in the hot caramel and when cool enough to handle roll them in the palm of your hand to form a cluster. Fill the top of each box with a cluster of hazelnuts. Holding the strawberries by the stalk, dip them in the caramel and let the caramel drip back in to form a long wand. Once the caramel has become hard, place 2 strawberries on each side of the nougatine boxes, crossing the wands.

 Don Ruinart Blanc de Blancs Vintage Champagne

hot and cold, dark and white chocolate plate

ingredients

150 g (5 oz) bitter dark chocolate

150 g (5 oz) unsalted butter

4 eggs

4 egg yolks

90 g (3 oz) Billington's golden natural caster sugar

20 g (¾ oz) flour, sieved

For the White Chocolate Sauce

250 ml (7 fl oz) milk

3 egg yolks

25 g (1 oz) Billington's golden natural caster sugar

25 g (1 oz) white chocolate, melted

For the Dark Chocolate Sauce

300 ml (½ pt) water

225 g (9 oz) Billington's golden natural sugar

95 g (3 oz) cocoa powder

115 g (4 oz) cream

SERVES 6

To make the hot chocolate dessert, finely cut the chocolate and melt it. Boil the butter. Have your eggs ready at room temperature and, in a mixer, combine them together with the caster sugar. Pour the boiling butter over the melted chocolate, and then add this to the egg and sugar, mixing on a medium speed. Fold in the flour and pour the mixture into 6 cm diameter buttered moulds before it sets. Once the mix is set it will keep.

To make the white chocolate sauce, first boil the milk. Combine the egg yolks and the sugar, and then add the hot milk to the egg mix. Cook over a bain-marie until it reaches a sauce-like consistency and then add the melted white chocolate.

To make the dark chocolate sauce mix all the ingredients and heat gently until you reach a sauce-like consistence. Strain and cool.

To serve, cook the set chocolate mix at 180°C/325°F/Gas Mark 4 for 10-12 minutes. Serve immediately with the sauces and some white chocolate ice cream.

 Banyuls Hors D'Age, Domaine de Valcros

Santa Carolina Reservado, Merlot, Chile.
- This excellent Merlot is grown in extensive vineyards near San Fernando, fermented in stainless steel tanks with some aging in French oak barrels. Rich and velvety with plum and prune flavours you can taste the heat of Chile, full bodied structure. Excellent with the brochette of lamb.

Dom Ruinart Blanc de Blancs Vintage Champagne
- Named after the Benedictine monk who observed the secret of "the wine which sparkles" from his friend Dom Pérignon. Dom Ruinart confided his knowledge to his nephew Nicolas Ruinart who in 1729 founded the first Champagne House. The vintage is matured in the Gallo-Roman cellars, old chalk pits made by the Romans when quarrying stone to build Reims and the distinctive bouquet comes from the blend of Côte des Blancs and the Montagne de Reims.

Santa Carolina Reservado, Sauvignon Blanc, Chile - The old winery is in the heart of Santiago and easy to visit. Sauvignon Blanc grapes from the Maipo Valley vineyards are fermented in stainless steel tanks to obtain a well balanced peach, fruity aroma, full bodied but dry working well with the sea bream dish.

Quincy Pierre Duret 1996 - This Sancerre style wine made from Sauvignon grapes from the Loire Valley has a fresh hay nose, with tastes of lemon and apricot and a well rounded finish. It is better value than the more well known Sancerre nearby. Matching the tartare of trout as well as a good wine to have before moving onto a heavier red.

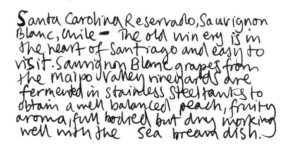

michel roux jnr

It was just before the lunch service at Le Gavroche. Two highly experienced sous chefs and the main sommelier were sitting at one of the beautifully laid tables with inveterate manager, Silvano Giraldin, and chef patron, Michel Roux Jnr. I had been invited to eat with them and was feeling just a little nervous. The restaurant has a certain gravity to it, a grand and formal standard against which other establishments are judged. The original Le Gavroche opened on Lower Sloane Street in Chelsea in 1967, the creation of Albert and Michel Roux. In 1981 it moved to its present location in Mayfair, a much bigger and different place altogether and, in 1982, the Michelin Guide awarded it three stars making it the first restaurant in the UK to achieve such an honour. The main dining room had undergone a substantial refurbishment with the help of Albert's wife, Monique Roux, and all was splendour in muted green and burgundy, contemporary table sculptures surrounded by opulent walls containing works by Picasso, Miro, Dali and Chagall.

That lunch was a few years ago. Now I feel I am an old hand, part of the team having, on many occasions, jostled for position with the chefs in the kitchen, perhaps with my face in the steam of a boiling pot as I strain to get a better angle for one of my pictures. I have eaten many an impromptu meal there, once a fine fish and chips, on a Friday, an off-cut of prize sea bass in batter – this, surely, is what life is all about. The approach to Le Gavroche's famous Upper Brook Street entrance is no longer a walk of trepidation, more one of recognition, especially

Richard Bramble 9.

after straining my eyes for weeks on end when painting every minute detail of the hundreds of red bricks for the restaurant's official 1995 Christmas card. If you look at the bricks for too long they start to move around – yes, it was the start of certain madness.

The evolution of Le Gavroche has been a steady process over thirty years and Michel Roux Jnr is a firm believer in not trying to change things overnight. When he took charge of the kitchen from the legendary Albert in 1991, he brought with him a deep respect for the classical foundations of French cooking having been 'born' into the tradition, as it were. But the Roux brothers were never ones to rest on their laurels, always keen to absorb new ideas and develop techniques that would make Le Gavroche one of the most consistently complete restaurants in London. Michel Jnr himself spent time in Hong Kong, experimenting with spices and ingredients, discovering ways to push the boundaries of classical French cooking without losing its identity.

Although the blueprint of fine cooking is rarely tampered with, the menu at Le Gavroche is looked at constantly. 'Experimentation happens every day,' Michel told me, 'it's ongoing, it happens all the time, not just physically or practically, but mentally, you're always thinking about it.'

Often I would be there when chefs would bring out new variations of the dishes, a new subtlety added to the sauce, or perhaps the main ingredient cooked in a slightly different way. It is scientific to a certain extent, certainly with pastry as everything has to be weighed out to the gram, but there is undeniably an art and a skill.

Some ingredients have changed over the years, for instance the more exotic spices from the East. Also, the growth in the number of suppliers has affected the industry with restaurants now enjoying a fantastic selection. Michel is enthusiastic. 'Europe is so big. Now, the "garden" is varied. A company I use goes to Italy twice a week, and France three times.'

With the greater variety there could, theoretically, be a problem with quality control. At Le Gavroche not only do the chosen suppliers have strict controls, but everything has to get past the man at the helm, Michel Roux Jnr.

Two generations of top chefs have come through Le Gavroche's kitchen on their road to success. Michel does not concern himself too much over the other personalities and their gastronomic inventions, however he does emphasise the importance of a chef eating out. 'Being a chef is eating out. When you're older, when you decide to stop moving, when you've experienced different environments, you no longer want to work in other restaurants. To broaden your ideas it's very important you eat out ... and not just the top restaurants. You need to experience different styles and foods, to keep you fresh. This is the only way a chef patron can keep his mind active in the field and not get into a rut.'

Michel's own background, though privileged, has not been an easy ride. Through washing dishes in his uncle's kitchen at The Waterside Inn he saved enough money to buy his first hi-fi system and racing bicycle at the age of thirteen. He was a keen cyclist at the time, thinking nothing of cycling to Brighton and back in a day. Michel left school at sixteen and went to France to spend two years doing a pastry apprenticeship, followed by a further two years' cooking apprenticeship. After this he did his military service working in the kitchens of the Elysée Palace. From there he went to work for Charcutier Mothu and La Boucherie Lamartine

in Paris before going to Hong Kong. Perhaps his greatest influence is that of Alain Chapel, whose restaurant at Mionnay is something of an historical landmark after five decades of existence.

Michel Roux Jnr now casts his own influence on the junior chefs at Le Gavroche, continuing and expanding the sorcery of his father's creations. Part of the seasonal menu still pays homage to Albert, but the rest is the new master's, lighter and perhaps more cosmopolitan, but with all the same sureness of taste. Equally, Michel has inherited his father's formidable management skills, running the kitchen with split-second precision. Time is critical: a lost minute can throw the whole service and tempers do flair. Michel leads from the front and every member of the staff is treated fairly and given the chance to grow. Once when I was there, a young commis chef came to Michel to get permission to leave for a dentist's appointment. Michel made the sound of a drill, smiled and told a joke, which managed to relax the poor white-faced fellow. He went on to tell me how chefs are prone to bad teeth, especially pastry chefs.

'You're not just tasting sweet things all the time, but you're breathing them in. Sugar's always in the air from the constant sifting ... so, the fact that you're breathing it in means you're constantly coating your teeth with the sugar ... terrible.' He laughed. 'Wine waiters get the same thing because they're constantly tasting the wine and wine rots their teeth something chronic ... the hazards of the restaurant trade.'

Michel takes care of his own body and manages to stay trim by running on Clapham Common close to his home or in Battersea Park; occasionally he goes fishing. He used to cycle to keep fit, but was banned by his wife because of

the dangers of venturing out in London traffic. After my scrape with a black cab I sympathise with his wife. One of Michel's favourite ways of spending any leisure time he has is to go to Disneyland in Paris with his wife Giselle and his daughter Emelie. Michel is fortunate at Le Gavroche in having a manager of the calibre of Silvano. Controlling a team of twenty-five, Silvano is the perfect complement to the pace and passion of the kitchen, putting the diner immediately at ease with a rare intelligence and unassuming confidence. A certain politician once wrote that if he needed a diplomat, he could not wish for anyone more qualified than Silvano Giraldin – charming and firm in equal and appropriate measure. I soon discovered his Wednesday evening ritual in which he gathers the staff round him in a semi-circle and gets them to recite the menu first in English, then in French. It is rather like watching a choirmaster warm up his singers before a performance. I once managed to disrupt the smooth running of his front of house. Because of my broken arm I was using the mahogany sorbet table to put my paints on. I had lost track of time and did not realise service was about to start. When Silvano politely asked for the table back I joked that he could not have it. His rarely-seen fiery temper put me in my place and I left with not only the pots of paint, but my tail between my legs. His anger never lasts long and the next day he was full of smiles as he helped me with the knot of my tie.

Another feather in the cap is the wine list: Le Gavroche was named the restaurant as having the best wine cellar in London by *American Wine Spectator* in 1997. There are over 20,000 bottles, with another 30,000 in bond, of a variety and quality few can match. Thierry, whom I have known since 1995, and four support sommeliers provide the interface between diner and liquid treasure.

I remember when I first asked Michel what he thought of my work. 'I like it. It's delicate, quite precise.' At the time, he had looked about the dining room and declared everything in it valuable. Then he stared at me. 'You still haven't given me one of your paintings ... all my staff have your prints.'

grass is always greener, but I don't want to end up here for ever. I have several ideas ... very personal. Slowly but surely, I'm coming round to writing a book, but it's in its embryonic stage ...' He cast me a wry smile. 'Is that right? My, that's a big word.' He laughed and leaned back in his chair

It would be a shame if Michel ever left – eating at Le Gavroche without a Roux running it would be like going to the Proms without 'Land of Hope and Glory'.

Most of the customers at the restaurant are regulars – often they write in to say something complimentary. Le Gavroche is moving with the times – the restaurant is on the internet through various guides. Indeed, food, fashion and design appear to be drawing closer together, at least in London. Michel realises this. 'There's a greater awareness of good things, of exciting things, which is good for London. And this lets the rest of the world know. Now, for example, the world knows it can come to London and eat interesting food.' He once told me that he finds it very difficult to pinpoint what cuisine he prefers. He does not appreciate the popular rise of fusion cooking and calls it 'confusion cooking', a cooking-by-numbers exercise that does not deserve the label modern British. Beyond doubt, there will never be any confusion at Le Gavroche as long as a Roux is in the kitchen.

I think it was a suggestion that I must have made a small fortune selling my work just within Le Gavroche. I thought it best to change the subject. 'I imagine you'll be wanting to run the ship for some time?'

'No. As soon as I can get out of this business the better.'

This came as a surprise. 'You have to be mad to do it. Obviously I enjoy the cooking, and the kitchen, but it's not a life is it?' I remained silent. 'I mean, I envy you. Yes, the

tajine of langoustine and cous-cous

ingredients

1 red pepper, peeled and diced

1 yellow pepper, peeled and diced

1 green pepper, peeled and diced

2 spring onions, thinly sliced

1 clove garlic, chopped

juice of 1 lime

1 dsp sultanas

1 red chilli, de-seeded and chopped

1.8 kilos (4 lb) langoustines, cooked and peeled

280 g (10 oz) cous-cous

extra virgin olive oil

salt and pepper

SERVES 6

Put the peppers into a hot frying pan with a little olive oil, reduce the heat and cook gently until tender. Add the garlic, chilli and sultanas, cook for a further minute, season and keep warm. Meanwhile, cook the cous-cous as per the packet instructions. Add a little olive oil, the spring onions and finally the lime juice. Keep warm.

To serve, place a neat pile of the pepper mix at the bottom of a heated tajine, followed by the cous-cous taking care to keep it light and fluffy. Place cooked langoustines on top and serve immediately.

 Condrieu 'Les Chaillets' Vieilles Vignes-Yves Cuilleron 1996

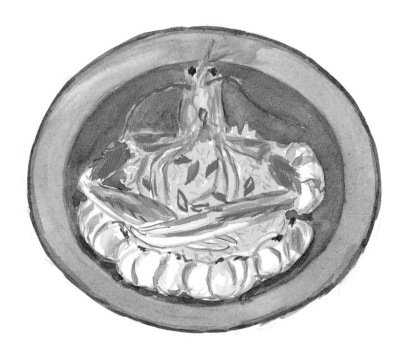

shoulder of milk lamb braised in saffron

ingredients

2 shoulders milk lamb, whole

3 plum tomatoes

1 generous pinch saffron

1 tsp cumin seeds

30 cocktail onions

3 cloves garlic, crushed

250 ml (8 fl oz) fresh orange juice

100 ml (3 fl oz) madiera

500 ml (16 fl oz) chicken stock

1 chilli, cut in half

olive oil

SERVES 3

Place the lamb shoulders in a wide pan and colour with a little olive oil on a high heat. Season with salt, add the cocktail onions and cook for a further 5 minutes, shaking the pan occasionally so that the onions do not burn. Add the garlic, saffron, chilli, tomatoes and cumin, then deglaze the pan with the madiera. Let this boil for a minute and then add the orange juice and stock. Simmer for approximately 40 minutes, or until tender and falling off the bone.

Leave to cool completely; even better, refrigerate for 24 hours. To serve, cut each shoulder into three along the joints and reheat in the sauce.

 Château Latour 1983 'Pauillac'

poulette de bresse en vessie

First, clean the chicken thoroughly and ensure there are no sharp bones protruding. Gently lift the skin from the breast and thigh using a little truffle oil to lubricate. Slide in the sliced truffles evenly. Place the chicken in the vessie and season well, then add a little madiera and 200 ml (7 fl oz) of the white chicken stock. Close the bag tightly with string. Poach in gently boiling water for an 1 hour 30 minutes.

Meanwhile, make the sauce by sweating the girolles until tender in a little butter, then deglaze with a splash of madiera and 100 ml (3 fl oz) of white chicken stock. Bring to the boil and reduce by a third. Now add the cream and the creme fraiche, and reduce once more until you have a sauce consistency.

When the chicken is cooked, remove from the water and leave to rest for about 10 minutes. Then take out of the vessie and carve. Garnish with the vegetables, lightly cooked to taste, and serve with the girolle sauce.

 Musigny Domaine Comte Georges de Vogue 1985

omelette rothschild

ingredients

For the Crème Patissière

250 ml (8 fl oz) milk

40 g (1½ oz) flour

60 g (2 oz) caster sugar

5 egg yolks

For the Marinated Apricots

20 dried apricots

250 ml (8 fl oz) water

150 g (5 oz) caster sugar

2 measures cointreau

For the Sauce

20 dried apricots

250 ml (8 fl oz) water

200 g (7 oz) sugar

4 vanilla pods

2 measures cointreau

For the Omelette

8 egg whites

1 dsp caster sugar

SERVES 4

First make the crème patissière by whisking the yolks and a third of the sugar until pale. Sift in the flour and mix well. Combine the milk with the remaining sugar in a pan and bring to the boil. As soon as the mixture bubbles, pour about a third onto the egg mix, stirring constantly. Return to the pan in which you have the rest of the milk mix, and gently bring to the boil, stirring constantly. Boil for two minutes, then transfer to a bowl and keep warm.

Next, prepare the marinated apricots. Boil the water and sugar, then pour it over the apricots. Add the Cointreau and leave to marinate.

Now make the sauce by boiling the sugar, apricots and the seeds from the vanilla pods in the water for 2 minutes. Add the cointreau and then blend for 2 minutes until a fine sauce consistency.

To prepare the omelettes, heat 4 blinis pans on the stove. Whisk the egg whites with the sugar until they form soft peaks, fold in half the crème patissièr until smooth (but without letting the egg whites down too much). Butter the pans and spoon in the mixture. Cook in the oven at 175°C/350°F/Gas Mark 4 for 6 minutes, turn out and serve with the hot sauce and marinated apricots.

 Jurançon 'Noblesse du Petit Manseng' Domaine Cauhape 1993

white chocolate and raspberry parfait

ingredients

4 egg yolks

1 tbsp caster sugar

4 egg whites

6 tbsp icing sugar

300 ml (½ pt) whipped cream

3 leaves gelatine

140 g (5 oz) white chocolate

30 g (1 oz) butter

2 drops vanilla essence

For the Raspberry Jelly

200 g (7 oz) raspberries

40 g (1½ oz) caster sugar

75 ml (2½ fl oz) red wine

1 leaf gelatine

Melt the chocolate and the butter in a bain-marie. Mix the yolks and the sugar together well, then add the vanilla. Dissolve the gelatine in a little cream and add this to the chocolate. Now mix the chocolate and the egg yolks, then the cream.

Make a meringue by beating the egg whites and icing sugar until they form soft peaks. Fold this into the mixture.

For the raspberry jelly, boil together the sugar and wine, then dissolve the gelatine into this. Pour the mixture over the raspberries. Leave to set.

Spoon a layer of the mousse into the bottom of an oval mould. Add a portion of the raspberry jelly and then a final layer of mousse. Leave in the fridge to set, and turn out when ready to serve.

 Vouvray Cuvée Constance S A Huet 1989

Vouvray Cuvée Constance S.A. Huet – A sweet wine from Le Loire, small production. S.A. Huet makes organic wine as well as picking and pruning according to the moon and sun cycles. Not too syrupy or sugary with lovely acidity. Can be drunk young but also with age.

Château Latour 1983 'Pauillac' – Creating some of the best red wines in the world because of the vines being of Grand Cru quality and the area – soil is very good and the wine with age develops a mushroomy gamey flavour. Flavours of 'tapenade' as well which gives some body to hold the dish of braised lamb.

Condrieu 'Les Chaillets' Vieilles Vignes – Yves Cuilleron 1996 – This white côte d'Rhone is quite spicy, flowery and powerful. It is made from the Viognier grape from the little vineyard 'Les Chaillets'. Small production.

Jurançon 'Noblesse du Petit Manseng' Domaine Canhapé 1993 – This sweet wine is from the South west of France. Not syrupy but spicey with a little apricot and exotic fruits. Good acidity at the back, and not too much sugar. The finish is quite long and very fresh. Small production, the 'Quintessence' of the grapes have been captured.

nico ladenis

Nico is now over sixty years old and does not cook in the kitchen any more because the stress is bad for his health. The cooking is left to the slightly more youthful head chefs, though Nico is never far away, always tasting the regular dishes and consulting, refining and creating new ones.

Nico Ladenis grew up in Africa, his playing fields a constantly changing and inspirational landscape. He was born in Tanzania to Greek parents. His father had decided to make a fresh start in Africa after owning a string of restaurants in America.

As a boy Nico remembers fishing on Lake Victoria and hunting gazelle on the plains. He went to school in the foothills of Mount Kilimanjaro before the family moved to the White Highlands of Kenya. He came to England to study economics at Hull University and ended up working for a major oil company in South America, but decided to leave when he was told he was 'non-conformist and argumentative'.

Nico has never lost something of the economist in him and keeps a tight check on the business side of the restaurant. Most mornings he can be found behind a desk in the reception, surveying the situation, his FT never far away – 'No FT, no comment'. Once I was part of an oversight that came close to sending every bell in his office ringing for a week. The sommelier, showing great trust, had lent me a bottle of Chateau d'Yquem so I could paint it for the wine notes. When I had finished, without thinking, I left it with one of the new waiters to be put back in the cellar. Subsequently, something distracted him and he left it in the kitchen where one of the commis chefs threw it, label hidden, among the unruly bottles of cooking wine. If it was not for the sharp eyes of the sous chef, there would have been some outrageously expensive stock the next day and I would have been painting for my supper, as it were.

Nico is a private man and quite difficult to talk to, at least I found it so ... unless you happen to be talking business. When I painted the outside picture of the restaurant – viewed from the central reservation in the middle of frantic Park Lane and subsequently featured in his book *Nico* – Nico initially wanted to buy it. His business acumen thought better of it, however, and he suggested that the Grosvenor House might get it for him as a Christmas present; finally, he hoped his wife might surprise him. In the end we were left to bash out a deal between the two of us. At the time I was quite desperate for cash, so I reduced the price of the painting and, as recompense, suggested a meal for four; Nico said two. Using all my negotiating skills, I said dinner. Nico's quick retort was 'lunch'. I said I would have to think about this. The result of my powers of

persuasion is that I have not got back to him, which has become something of a joke between us. Another time I met him was one April Fools' Day. He was pacing up and down the deep-pile reception carpet like a caged tiger, upset by a reservation he had just noticed. 'Who is this Mr Squirrel? I'm sure it's an April Fools' … we must check.'

It turned out that there was a genuine Mr Squirrel. I found it all rather amusing, but Nico had the attitude that a man with the name of Squirrel had no right making a table reservation on April Fools' Day. Nico can be rather serious at times.

Chez Nico has a history of 29 years, Nico and Dinah-Jane, his wife, on returning from a sabbatical in the South of France, and having developed a taste for good food, decided to open their own restaurant. Eventually, in 1973, Chez Nico opened its doors to Lordship Lane in East Dulwich. Apparently, the only thing going for the place at the time was a low rent; by pure will alone, and with a certain amount of his famous arrogance, Nico made it work. From day one he took a tough stand, giving the customer what he thought they ought or ought not to have, for example his 'no well-done steaks'. He created an identity by, unwittingly, adopting an approach of exclusivity long before the advertising industry was using it. Even if he had an empty restaurant he would turn people away if they had not booked. Word soon got round that you had to make a reservation at Chez Nico because it only used the freshest ingredients available and the chef needed to know what to buy. Irrespective of how many diners they were actually receiving, rumour spread that this was the place to be.

The enterprise was helped by a family team

effort, Dinah-Jane looking after the front of house and their two daughters, Natasha and Isabelle, helping in all areas as they grew up. Natasha originally wanted to go to art school. She started a course, but was called in to help with the restaurant and only recently left to join Marks & Spencer as a specialist food consultant buyer. As one artist to another she took a personal interest in this project.

As he started reading about Michelin-starred chefs and meeting some of them, including Michel Roux, Nico realised that he would never be taken seriously in the suburbs. In 1979 he converted a burnt-out café and Chez Nico moved to Battersea, doing battle with the locals before winning the first star in 1981. A second star followed in 1984. In search of a third, and grander surroundings, Chez Nico moved again to an old rectory in Shinfield near Reading – Nico left after only a year, missing his regular London audience, and leaving room for John Burton-Race to move in with L'Ortolan. Chez Nico next found itself in Rochester Row, Victoria. But the space was far too small and Nico found another unusual location just north of Oxford Street in Great Portland Street. He was one of the first chefs to convert his former premises into a 'gastronomic bistro' called Simply Nico. Nico finally found his ultimate 'grand location' when he took over the luxury dining room of the Grosvenor House Hotel on Park Lane. He converted Great Portland Street into yet another Bistro called Nico Central. He sold them both to Roy Ackerman who is expanding both the names into a large chain of Brasseries from Manchester to Brussels.

The new Chez Nico was an instant success and allowed Nico to reach the dizzy heights he had always aspired to. He now had a staff of forty and was hosting up to eighty guest diners in his new spacious and elegant dining room. In 1995, after eleven years at two star level, he was awarded the top prize of three Michelin stars. In 2000, under the capable hands of executive group chef Paul Rhodes, Nico opened the now highly successful Incognico, in central London, the name being a play on words, with Nico out of the kitchen and in the background. In 2002 due to building work work at Grosvenor House Hotel, the Ladenises decided not to renew the lease on Chez Nico and now base them selves at the new flagship restaurant Deca, appropriately named as the tenth restaurant Nico has opened.

In his book, *Nico,* the uncompromising chef has always said he has been guided by three things: precision, restraint and simplicity.

Do not be led astray by over elaborate garnishes or clashing flavours. Do not experiment every time you start to cook ... The quest for perfection will lead you to role models that will last you for life.

'Crocus sativus'   'Saffron flower'

Saffron is made up of the tiny orange-red stigmas from the flower of 'Crocus Sativus'. A beautiful purple, lily shaped crocus growing some six inches in height. It takes over 150,000 saffron flowers to produce one kilogram of saffron making it the most expensive spice in the world. Since the Middle Ages the best has come from the plains of Iran and La Mancha in Spain. The corms (bulbs) are planted in July and the flowers gathered in September. In the evenings whole families work together removing the stigmas by hand. These are then dried in a kiln then pressed to form flat cakes.

Mentioned in the song of Solomon, saffron was loved by the phoenicians, who carried it along the mediterranean coast to France. There is a story that they also took it to Cornwall and traded it for tin, so starting the Cornish love of saffron cake. Saffron was first taken to the United States by a German called Schwenfelder, who grew it on a fairly large scale in Pennsylvania. In America, saffron cake is called Golden Schwenfelder cake.

Prized for its colour as well as its taste, saffron dyed shoes were once worn by Persian Kings and the dye is still used for the robes of Buddhist monks. Many countries of the world have their own special recipes using saffron. There is the Spanish paella, the French bouillabaisse and the Italian risotto. From India there is saffron rice and from Iran a yellow rice pudding called 'Sholezard'. Jewish cookery has 'challah', a plaited bread and 'gildeme', a chicken soup made for sabbaths, holidays and weddings.

mussel soup with saffron

ingredients

120 g (4 oz) butter

2 tbsp olive oil

½ onion, diced

½ leek, diced

1 carrot, diced

1 small bunch of parsley

4 cloves garlic, chopped

2 sprigs fresh tarragon

salt and pepper

1 l (1 pt 13 fl oz) mussels, well cleaned

1 bottle dry white wine

400 ml (13 fl oz) double cream

1 small sachet saffron

1 tbsp chives, chopped

SERVES 4

Melt the butter with the olive oil in a large frying pan and sauté the diced vegetables until soft. Add the parsley, garlic and tarragon with a little salt and plenty of pepper. Cook for a few more minutes, stirring well.

Pour the wine into a large saucepan and throw in the mussels, cooking until they open. Leave to cool. When they have cooled, strain, reserving the liquid and remove the mussels from their shells. Pass the reserved liquid through several layers of muslin, ensuring all sediment is discarded. Pick out the best mussels and set aside. Place the remaining mussels in the pan containing the vegetables and pour in the strained liquid. Simmer for 20 minutes. Tip the contents into a sieve and press well to extract the juices. Put the liquid into a clean saucepan, add the cream. Bring to the boil and add the saffron. Simmer for a few minutes, stirring well, and skim if necessary.

Add the reserved mussels and sprinkle with chives

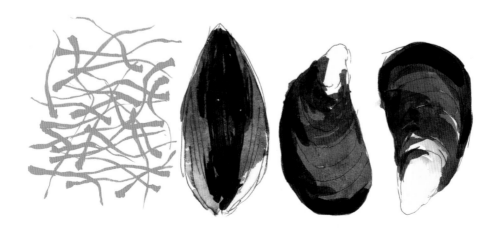

chicken with vin jaune

ingredients

4 corn-fed chicken legs

36 plump dried morels

flour seasoned with salt and pepper

225 g (8 oz) butter

300 ml (½ pt) vin jaune

600 ml (1 pt) double cream

SERVES 2

Pour very hot water over the dried morels, and leave to soak for 40 minutes. Dust the chicken legs in a little seasoned flour. In a heavy non-stick frying pan, seal the chicken in butter without browning. Arrange the chicken legs in a roasting pan with a lid, pouring over the buttery juices from frying.

Cook in a preheated oven at 175°C/350°F/Gas Mark 4 for 20 minutes. Make sure that the legs are not browning. Drain the butter from the pan. Place it over a medium heat and add the morels with a little of the soaking liquid. Pour over the vin jaune, followed by the cream. The sauce should be syrupy enough to coat the chicken.

Arrange the chicken legs on a plate. Removing the morels, pass the sauce through a sieve. Gently reheat the sauce and spoon over the chicken legs. Arrange the morels in mounds on top of each chicken leg.

walnut and raisin bread

ingredients

640 g (1 lb 7 oz) strong white flour

260 g (9 oz) strong brown flour

6 g sachet of easy blend yeast

600 ml (1 pt) tepid water

50 g (1¾ oz) raisins

50 g (1¾ oz) shelled walnuts

1 tsp of sea salt

spray bottle of water

SERVES 8

Put the water and yeast in a bowl and mix in the flour gradually with an electric mixer at the lowest setting. Use a dough hook if you have one. The dough mixture should be about 40°C/105°F – you can reach this by changing the water temperature. Be careful if you are using a high protein flour as the heavy dough can burn out some mixers. Mix for 10 minutes. If the dough is pulling apart in strands, add more water, if it is too moist, add more flour. Mix in the salt and sugar and switch the mixer to full for 2 minutes.

The dough should be elastic, bouncing back when it is pressed down. Mix in the raisins and walnuts. Then shape the dough into a ball on a floured surface. If you prefer a lighter bread keep the dough in a zip lock bag in the fridge for 24 hours, before bringing to room temperature and allowing to rise.

Place in a large bowl, brush the bowl and top of the dough with olive oil to prevent it from sticking, and cover loosely with cling film. Leave at room temperature for at least 4 hours until it has doubled in size.

Knead for 3 minutes, then shape and dust with flour. Place on a thick baking sheet or tin and spray with water. Put into an oven preheated to 220°C/425°F/Gas Mark 7, generously sprayed with water to generate steam. Alternatively, you can splash an espresso cup of water into the hot oven. Bake for 20 minutes. Turn onto a wire rack to cool.

sorbets with lime syrup

ingredients

For the Cassis Sorbet

500 ml (17 fl oz) water

500 g (1 lb 2 oz) caster sugar

125 g (4 oz) frozen blackcurrants

150 ml (5 fl oz) crème de cassis

a little lemon juice

For the Passion Fruit Sorbet

45 passion fruits

600 ml (1 pt) water

400 g (14 oz) caster sugar

a little lemon juice

For the Lemon Sorbet

500 ml (17 fl oz) water

330 g (11 oz) caster sugar

zest and juice of five lemons

For the Lime Syrup

zest of 8 limes

200 g (7 oz) caster sugar

200 ml (7 fl oz) water

juice of 3 limes

For the cassis sorbet, bring the sugar and the water to the boil and simmer for 15 minutes. Pour the syrup onto the blackcurrants. Liquidise and pass through a sieve, making sure all seeds have been removed. Stir in the crème de cassis. Add a squeeze of lemon before freezing. Stir while freezing.

For the passion fruit sorbet, scoop out juice, seeds and membranes. Liquidise the passion fruit pulp and pass through a fine sieve. Make a sugar syrup as above, and pour the syrup over the strained pulp. Leave to cool, before freezing. Stir while freezing as before.

For the lemon sorbet, make a sugar syrup as before. Tip all the lemon zest into the syrup to infuse as it cools. Add the lemon juice. Strain the contents through a fine sieve. Place in a freezer, regularly stirring as it freezes.

For the lime syrup, blanch the zest three times. Place zest in a saucepan with the sugar and water. Bring to the boil and simmer for 30 minutes. Remove from the heat and leave to infuse for 1 hour. Strain the lime juice and add to the syrup, then pass through a wet tammis cloth.

rum babas

ingredients

250 g (9 oz) plain flour

15 g (½ oz) fresh yeast

425 ml (14 fl oz) lukewarm water

125 g (4½ oz) melted butter

4 eggs

a pinch of salt

a pinch of caster sugar

rum

For the Deluxe Stock Syrup

juice of 1 lemon

juice of 1 orange

250 g (9 oz) caster sugar

500 ml (17 fl oz) water

½ cinnamon stick

1 vanilla pod

For the Apricot Glaze

250 g (9 oz) apricot jam

125 ml (4 fl oz) water

MAKES ABOUT 40

First make the deluxe stock syrup by putting all the ingredients into a pan and bringing to the boil. Simmer for about 15 minutes, remove from the heat, cover and leave to infuse until completely cold. Pass through a sieve.

Now sieve the flour into a large bowl and add the salt and sugar. Dissolve the yeast in the water and add to the flour. Whisk the eggs into the flour and slowly add the butter and beat for about 5 minutes until the dough tightens and all the butter is absorbed. Lightly butter your petits fours moulds and half-fill with the mixture. Leave until it has doubled in size, and then bake in an oven preheated at 175°C/350°F/Gas Mark 4 for 15 minutes. Remove from the oven and leave to cool.

Soak the babas in warm sugar syrup and sprinkle liberally with rum. Make an apricot glaze by heating the water and the apricot jam in a saucepan until well combined. Pass through a fine sieve and then use to coat the rum babas.

A selection of petits fours, of which the rum baba is served as one

tom aikens

Tom Aikens is a man with a mission. Every time I have seen him he looks exhausted, rarely surfacing from the kitchen of his own restaurant in Chelsea. Indeed, Tom is one of the few head chefs who still frequently peels the vegetables himself. During his stint at Pied à Terre, where he gained his legendary reputation, sometimes the extractor fan broke down and the temperature would rise above fifty degrees, causing the less hardy members of his nine-strong brigade to teeter on the verge of fainting. If Tom was ill, the restaurant closed. But the food, even the simplest items on the menu, was always exquisite. My weakness was continually to grab a chunk of home-made rosemary bread and pair it with some of the fine cheese which is sent over from Strasbourg twice a week.

A small place in town for occasional use: this is what everyone understands by pied à terre which, directly translated, means 'foot on (the) ground'. You would never guess to look at it, but Pied à Terre was once an Indian restaurant. Due to a tight budget, improvisation has always been the underpinning theme. Its style was born

out of Pied à Terre having no money when it opened and the Indian restaurant having a minimalist look. So, minimalism was embraced, nothing was thrown away and an ad hoc refurbishment was undertaken. The original 'frosted' window was actually ordinary glass varnished by running a roller over it – 'everyone thought we were terribly swish'. The effect works, especially when seen from the outside at night, the glass alive with the gentle colours of the restaurant and its diners, glowing and enticing, reminiscent of a fine painting revealing itself over time. To compare, the new frosted glass costs a cool £4,000. It is a valuable lesson to learn just what you can do without money. Tom remains as shrewd now that the restaurant is a success as he was at the beginning, and continued going to Covent Garden Market himself to buy his own produce and save the pennies.

Tom Aikens first became inspired by food when his father, who was in the wine business, bought a barn in France for frequent family holidays. A typical day might have been visiting a vineyard, spending the afternoon with a few of his father's French friends, then eating at a fantastic local restaurant far away from tourist routes. Tom describes his mother as a good cook, his father as a good businessman, but able to cook nothing other than a boiled egg. Tom did not cook at home. An obvious career for Tom would have been to follow in his father's – and his grandfather's – footsteps and enter the wine trade. Instead, he made up his mind to go his own way and enrolled at Norwich College to study cooking. He did well and, after leaving Norwich, went to a 'basic' restaurant in Eastbourne for eighteen months. Soon after his twenty-first birthday, Tom left for London and started writing letters to restaurants in the hope of a job. David Cavalier offered him a six week unpaid trial period at Cavalier's, a Michelin-starred restaurant with a menu biased towards fish and offal. It was an eye-opener for Tom when he finally got on the payroll only to find himself preparing vegetables from seven in the morning until one the following morning. If this was not *Down and Out in Paris and London* it was certainly close. Tom found it hard to keep at it and things were not made easier by his living arrangements. At the time he had a mortgage with his twin brother. 'He had a cushy job working for the Roux brothers' corporate catering operation ... he finished at three in the

afternoon! Then our cousin moved in. She was a model and used to bring round all these beautiful girls. I'd be slaving away in the kitchen thinking about my brother off having fun.'

In the end Tom got so frustrated with his hours he walked out. The next day he received a phone call from David Cavalier asking him to go back in for a talk. 'David told me I could take it one of two ways. I could find an easy place to work and have a great social life, but in ten years' time where would I be? Or, I could decide to get my head down, do the hard work and have something to show for it. I chose to go back.'

After Cavalier's, Tom went to The Capital Hotel to work under Philip Britten for a short fixed term before moving on to Pierre Koffman's La Tante Claire with its predominantly French staff. 'It was the most enjoyable place I have worked. Pierre's incredibly dedicated … he's a nice guy, but he really speeds you up. When I was on the fish he used to come over and give me races. He has had the most influence on my cooking, but there's only so much you can pick up from other people … there's always the little things you'll do yourself. Some time after I'd left I was passing and went to the kitchen to say hello. I was a real scruff-bag, hair all over the place, ripped jeans, but Pierre took me to the restaurant, sat me next to some considerably smarter-looking diners and gave me a five-course lunch consisting of all his signature dishes.'

Pied à Terre was co-founded in December 1991 by current manager, David Moore, and previous chef, Richard Neat. David and Richard hatched their plans at Le Manoir aux Quat' Saisons where they were both working under Raymond Blanc. Blanc was very much involved at first, but when Neat left twenty-nine months later after winning two Michelin stars, Blanc decided to walk away, too.

Before Neat's departure, Aikens went to work at Pied à Terre, finding the kitchen very particular in the way it did things and very pressured because of the confined space. The time was still not right for Tom's permanent residency in Charlotte Street and he went to Paris to work for Joël Robuchon for ten months. If he thought the hours at Cavalier's were bad, he was in for a rude awakening. 'It was crazy … the hours were from 5.30 a.m. until after 1.00 a.m. all the way through apart from a fifteen minute break at four o'clock. I used to get home at two in the morning, too tired to sleep, just lying there thinking I had to be up again in a few hours to do it all again.'

This really was Orwellian. When the great chef retired, Tom returned to London. Within five months Richard Neat had left Pied à Terre and Tom Aikens found himself installed as head chef

with the unenviable task of retaining two Michelin stars in a restaurant where all but two of the staff had walked out with Neat. 'There was just me, David and another guy ... three of us for six months!'

Tom never had one dish he prefered at Pied à Terre, but notes that the braised pig's head was ordered quite a lot.

Both Tom and David made it a point of eating out in other top restaurants, abroad as often as possible. David once took Tom to a restaurant in Spain. 'I took him to El Bulli in Rosas, North Barcelona, a three star Michelin restaurant with the best setting I have ever seen. It is on a mountain and you approach it by a dirt track road, which eventually turns a corner to reveal

a panorama of the ocean below. They have a space-age kitchen and the chef is like the Salvador Dali of cuisine … his food is out of this world, the old classics done completely differently … the most fabulous food I've eaten in my life. Tom just sat there amazed .. and that was the canapés!'

Social life takes a back seat for Tom and

David, though both have found the time to get married. It took me a while to get used to the new 'clean cut' David after he shaved off his goatee beard because he did not want it stamped for ever in his wedding photographs. In 2000 Tom and David went their separate ways. With the capable Shane Osborn, who refined his cooking skills at The Square with Philip Howard, Pied à Terre continued and retained a Michelin star.

Tom is married to Laura who was Pied à Terre's assistant manager. It was Laura over the last couple of years who helped Tom find the right premises to open their own restaurant, Tom Aikens, due to open in early 2003. Situated on Elystan Street in the heart of Chelsea, it will allow Tom to pursue his passion for cooking and the public once again to taste his creations. Tom and his twin brother, Rob, have always had a dream of owning their own restaurant, and without a doubt it would be a huge success. But then if Tom's phenomenal success is anything to go by, so will Tom Aikens, in the heart of Chelsea.

boudin of guinea fowl

ingredients

2 guinea fowl legs, boned

150 g (5 oz) fresh ceps, diced into 1cm cubes

150 g (5 oz) veal sweetbreads, diced into 1cm cubes

100 g (3½ oz) fresh foie gras

100g (3½ oz) chicken mousse

10 g (½ oz) parsley, finely chopped

70 g (2 oz) unsalted butter

1 l (1¾ pt) duck fat

plain flour

salt and pepper

SERVES 4

Season and flour the sweetbread cubes. Melt the butter in a pan until golden brown, add the sweetbreads and when golden all over add the ceps. Cook for 5 minutes. Season, drain off the butter and allow to cool.

Purée the foie gras in a mixer and pass through a fine sieve. In a bowl, lightly mix together the sweetbreads, ceps, parsley, chicken mousse and foie gras. Season.

Using a piping bag with a large opening, pipe the mix into both the guinea fowl legs. Roll the legs in a sheet of cling film and tie at both ends. Repeat with a second layer of cling film, again tying both the ends. Place the boudins into a pan of melted duck fat and cook over a low heat for 3 hours.

Remove the boudins from the fat and allow to cool a little. While still warm, remove the cling film and wrap with a new sheet of cling film to help them to keep their shape. Leave to cool completely (they can be kept in the fridge for a couple of days).

Serve slices of the boudin cold with a salad of haricots verts and asparagus.

 Gewürztraminer 1994 Grand Cru Kitterlé Domaine Schlumberger

venison fillet with beetroot gratin and beetroot purée

SERVES 4

ingredients

4 fillets of venison, approx
100 g (3½ oz) each

1 tbsp olive oil

10 g (¼ oz) butter

4 sprigs rosemary

half a lemon

For the Beetroot Purée

3 beetroot

250 ml (8 fl oz) port

50 g (2 oz) butter

For the Beetroot Gratin

3 beetroot, peeled and
finely sliced

1 large baking potato, peeled
and finely sliced

1 sprig thyme

1 bulb garlic, split in half

300 ml (½ pt) cream

For the Herb Breadcrumbs

4 slices white bread

handful of flat leaf parsley

1 sprig rosemary

1 clove garlic

First make the beetroot purée. Peel and chop the beetroot into 1 cm cubes. Sweat in a pan with the butter with the lid for 15-20 minutes until the beetroot is soft. Do not allow the beetroot to colour. Add the port and reduce slowly until only 2 tbsp liquid remains. Purée, and pass through a fine sieve.

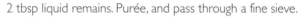

For the beetroot gratin, add the garlic and thyme to the cream and heat together. Take off the heat and leave for 20 minutes. Pass through a chinois and reserve the cream. Layer the beetroot and the potato with the cream and seasoning in an ovenproof dish until 3 cm deep. Cook at 200°C/400°F/Gas Mark 6 for 30 minutes

Next, make the herb breadcrumbs. Cut the crusts off the bread and dry out in a very low oven. Process it to a fine crumb and pass the crumb through a fine sieve. Finely chop the herbs and garlic and then chop with the breadcrumbs in a food processor.

Seal the venison in a hot pan with the oil and butter. Remove from the pan and wrap up each fillet in cling film with a sprig of rosemary. Tie the ends and steam for 5-7 minutes. Leave to rest for 10 minutes.

Reheat the beetroot purée. Now unwrap the rested venison and reheat for 2 minutes in a hot oven at 200°C/400°F/Gas Mark 6. Roll in a little beetroot purée and the herb crumb. Place some beetroot gratin in the centre of a plate. Slice each fillet in two and place on the top. Serve with a port wine sauce.

 Gevrey Chambertin Premier Cru 1992 Claude Dugat

lime parfait with ginger savarin

SERVES 4

ingredients

zest and juice of 3 limes

5 egg yolks

90 g (3 oz) caster sugar

180 ml (6 fl oz) double cream

For the Lime Syrup

zest and juice of 2 limes

12 g (½ oz) caster sugar

For the Ginger Savarin

100 g (3 oz) soft butter

100 g (3 oz) icing sugar

80 g (3 oz) plain flour

45 g (1½ oz) ground almonds

2 eggs

1 tsp ground ginger

6 g (¼ oz) stem ginger, finely diced

To make the lime parfait, add the lime juice to the sugar and bring to the boil. Boil for 3 minutes until you have a thick clear syrup. Meanwhile, whisk the egg yolks to double their volume and then slowly pour on the hot lime syrup, whisking constantly. Whisk until cold. Now, lightly whip in the cream and fold it into the egg yolks with the lime zest. Place the mixture into a rectangular tray, approx 30 cm x 20 cm x 1.5 cm (12 in x 8 in x in). Freeze for approximately 2 hours until the parfait is set.

Meanwhile, make the lime syrup by putting all the ingredients in a pan and bringing to the boil. Remove from the heat and leave to cool.

Now, make the ginger savarin. Beat together the butter, sugar, flour, almonds and eggs until fully incorporated. Mix in the stem ginger and the ground ginger.

To serve, half fill 4 individual small round moulds with the savarin mixture. Cook at 200°C/400°F/Gas Mark 6 for 5-8 minutes until firm to the touch. Cut the lime parfait into triangles, 3 per person. Turn out the warm savarins. Serve the individual savarins with three triangles of lime parfait on top. Pour a little lime syrup around.

 Mumm Cramant Blanc de Blancs Champagne

Gevrey Chambertin 1er Cru 1992, Claude Dugat – From the tiny domaine in the Côte d'Or, Claude Dugat make wines of the highest class in the picturesque Cellier des Dîmes. They are organic, weeds compete with the vines making them grow deeper and creating a small concentrated grape. The yield is small so production is low but very good. The region is young and not gamey so this fine, subtle, fruity red Burgundy made from the Pinot Noir grape is a good match.

Meursault 1992 1er Cru Chevaliere Domaine Coche-Dury – Jean-Francois Coche-Dury is the third generation to own this Côte d'Or 21 acre domaine, with powerful oaky, yet wonderfully balanced wines. This is a rich well structured full flavoured white Burgundy. A young vintage 1992 has been chosen to give added acidity to pair with the sea bass' creamy sauce. It has the finesse to go with the fish along with the fullness so as not to be drowned by the Oyster beignets.

Gewürztraminer 1994 Grand Cru Kitterlé Domaine Schlumber – The biggest domaine in the Alsace, family owned, half the estate is of Grand Cru vineyards. Guebwiller's warm climate, sandy soil allied with old style methods ageing in wood make their wines some of the richest and roundest in Alsace, with sweet earthy flavours of their own. This wine comes from the Kitterlé vineyard – the best and – repays several years bottle ageing being spicy and full bodied, qualities needed to pair with the asparagus and ceps in the Boudin dish.

Mumm Cramant, Blanc de Blancs Champagne – made from Chardonnay grapes of a single year from the village of Cramant. This fruity champagne with no hint of oak has a very full flavour which will compete with the tartness of the lime, whilst the fizz will counter the creaminess of the parfait.

philip howard

I used to consider myself in good condition; I used to get on to the squash court regularly. Philip Howard runs marathons in his spare time – he's just plain fit. 'I run like a mad man,' Philip told me when I went back to his restaurant to finish off some pictures and to hand over some money for a previous run for which I had sponsored him. 'The Barbados Marathon is coming up,' he continued, 'and New York.'

When I was at The Square, Philip had already collected £7,000 through his running for charities and causes that are close to his heart. He finds the New York Marathon a lot harder because the grid system is monotonous with eight mile straights 'somewhat boring'. His fastest marathon was in London in 1997, crossing the finishing line in 3 hours 36 minutes. He trains every day, in the park in the summer, in the gym in the winter. He says he feels good for the first twenty miles, but the last five are quite a different matter. He has never had a running injury, but broke both his ankles jumping off a sea wall in Australia at the start of a year travelling after university. He was in a wheelchair for a week and, miraculously, his ankles recovered and are now as good as new. When Philip Howard is not running, he is master chef at The Square, a glamorous two-star restaurant which opened in 1991 and has since moved from its original St James's location to Bruton Street. Now the food is refinement at its best; in the beginning Howard admits he was tempted to run wild. Philip Howard has never been one to opt for the safe route.

Howard first experimented with food at university, where he lived with a 'vegetarian anthropologist' and a 'German vegan'. He remembers really enjoying the cooking, even if the result was often quirky. When he finished his degree he had some dead time before he took his gap year and went travelling. He decided to go to

France to immerse himself in a restaurant in the Dordogne. 'It was a simple kitchen, part of a language school in a chateau where my parents had won a competition to learn French.'

Even though the cuisine was basic, cooking had impressed itself upon him and Philip went off on his travels with a feeling of what he wanted to do with his life. By strange coincidence a friend of his whom I met at a dinner party told me the story of how he made up his mind. Having spent enough time away from it all, he was sitting by a fire he had built next to his camper van when he made a decision – perhaps the best he has ever made – to follow his instincts. 'I decided to be a cook. I was worried about what my father would say ... he'd just spent God knows how many thousands of pounds on a private education, I'd gone to university, come out with a degree in microbiology, had already been accepted by a couple of pharmaceutical companies and here I was about to do something completely different that had nothing remotely to do with my studies and training. I told him from Australia ... I wrote him a postcard ... it was pathetic. And his response was one of total support ... he thought it was brilliant.'

Howard still found the whole world of microbiology fascinating, but once he had made up his mind to cook he really went for it. When he returned from his adventures he spent two weeks composing a letter to the top twenty restaurant establishments he would like to work in. 'I was going against all odds because I didn't have any experience ... some people said "get back to where you came from".'

He eventually got a job with the Roux brothers in their contract catering operation and spent a year there learning a dish a day. He says he left before he got too 'moulded' and got his first 'proper job' working at Harvey's, Marco Pierre White's restaurant in Wandsworth. 'Everything went incredibly well until Marco sacked me.'

Marco changed his mind and asked him back, but Philip decided to keep on moving. 'It was exhausting at Harvey's, but I learnt a lot ... I learnt what was possible. Imagine the energy that Marco gives to all his restaurants now, chanelled into just one restaurant then. It was phenomenal. It will never be repeated, a bit like The Beatles and The Rolling Stones in the sixties. Now, there are too many good restaurants around.'

From Harvey's Howard went to Bibendum. 'I had seen the refined classical style of the Roux brothers, then the more modern version of it with Marco ... next I wanted to experience some real gutsy food ... that's why I went to Bibendum.'

He was there for just over a year, constantly impressed by Simon Hopkinson's cooking. 'Simon is someone who can cook something simple with great finesse. To charge nine pounds for aubergine with pesto you have to understand what it's about ... a lot of people missed the point.'

Philip was happy there, but it was also a time in his life when he wanted to gain more responsibility. The opportunity came when Nigel Platts-Martin (the owner of Harvey's who launched Marco) asked him to be head chef at his new restaurant on St James's Square. 'I was grossly unprepared to take charge ... it was unrealistic, really.'

So, way before his time, Philip Howard was in charge of The Square, starting off as an employee but eventually becoming a partner with Platts-Martin. They got a star after about three years, which surprised everyone as it was the first restaurant of its kind to get such an accolade – until then all Michelin-starred places were normally very 'deluxe'. He also struggled more than most due to a lack of management skills and not enough experience, but they knew they were doing the right thing. 'I suppose seven years ago there wasn't the competition there is now ... we struck the right vein at the right time. It was also the toughest time of my life ... it really took its toll, to be honest. I was not running then ... I was not doing anything outside of the work ... I was snared. It was a hard bit of life which took its toll in many ways, including on my marriage ... that's a massive regret.' (There is a happy ending as the couple are now back together.)

In his early cooking years he used to eat out mostly in fine restaurants – 'My wife has a wonderful palate.' He still enjoys eating refined food, but generally prefers the more relaxed places. He does not follow exactly a traditional French cuisine, but is a purist in the sense that he respects classical combinations. There is nothing remotely extreme or quirky about the food at The Square, though this does not mean he will not inject some modern twists, taking a traditional dish, for example, breaking it down into its various components, then rebuilding it into a fine and delicate one. 'You must always respect the basic components. Man has been eating for millions of years ... years of trying and testing ... what we have now is what works well. There are underlying rules that point to what is right and wrong.'

Of course, the positive side of gaining Michelin stars is unquestionable, helping to attract better staff and to create a niche in London's top restaurants. When I was last there he had just arrived from blowing glass all morning with the artist who makes various vases and dessert dishes for the restaurant. If you know where to look you will find his Aston Martin DB7 parked outside. 'I went from a Fiat Panda to an awesome Bristol 411,' he told me, 'which I couldn't afford to run at the time, so I went back to something smaller and got a Renault Clio. Now I have an Aston Martin.'

It is all part of his new search for balance in his life, to enjoy the fruits of his hard work. Like me, he also goes fly fishing. His father has a stretch on the River Test, and when I last spoke with him about it, Philip had bought a small smoker with the idea of smoking some of his catch at the restaurant.

'You have to have variety in what you do. When I first started with The Square I lost touch with friends ... it was hard, my social life was right on my doorstep, yet I didn't have contact. I've really concentrated in the last couple of years to get back in contact with people.'

Most importantly, he makes sure he gives priority to spending time with his wife, Jennie, and his young daughter Millie. Even though he might now enjoy a more balanced life, Philip will always be in the kitchen for the lunch and dinner services, supporting his brigade of 18 in the kitchen. He came out the first time I had dinner there. We discussed plates and I went on to design some hand-painted ones for the private dining room – at the moment these original designs hang on the walls at Philip's home, though I hope the restaurant eventually uses them as plates because they are some of my favourite work.

Despite the success of The Square, Philip has resisted the temptation of getting involved in outside consultancies so that he can maintain his focus on The Square. Philip Howard's vision for the future is for The Square to be around for a long time, for it to be one of the great restaurants in London.

marinated seabass with tuna, crab and coriander

ingredients

300 g (10½ oz) fillet of seabass

200 g (7 oz) tuna loin

100 g (3½ oz) fresh white crab meat

For the Seabass Marinade

30 g (1 oz) salt

15 g (½ oz) sugar

zest and juice of 1 lime

½ bunch of coriander

1 star anise

½ red chilli

For the Crab

½ lime

1 tsp coriander, chopped

1 tsp olive oil

salt and pepper

For the Garnish

¼ leek

¼ carrot

¼ raw beetroot

¼ white radish

cut all the above into julliennes

SERVES 4

First marinate the seabass. Wash the piece of seabass. Blend all the ingredients for the marinade in a food processor to a pulp. Stretch out a large piece of cling film on the work surface and spread onto it the marinade to the size of the piece of fish. Lay the bass on top and cover with the remaining half of the marinade. Fold the cling film over and place in the fridge for 4 hours. Then rinse, pat dry and place in the freeezer, along with the tuna, to firm up. This should take about an hour.

Season the juliennes of vegetables with salt, pepper, lime juice and olive oil and place in the fridge.

Cut the seabass into 12 thin slices, cutting with a sharp, wet knife, slightly on the angle. Similarly, cut the tuna into 12 slices, but cut straight down. Dress the crab with the lime, coriander, olive oil, salt and pepper.

On each of 4 chilled plates, arrange alternately, in a circle, 3 slices of tuna and 3 slices of seabass. In the middle, put a pile of crab and top with a nest of the juliennes of vegetables. Then, if desired, drizzle the plates with a light vinaigrette.

 Sancerre Pinot Noir Vacheron 1995, Loire

Wild Mushrooms

Two hundred years ago British market places were bursting with people selling wild mushrooms. Lost over time, this tradition of the so called 'peasant' ingredient has been elevated to its rightful status once more with the revival in British Gastronomy. With this revival comes a need to educate people on the correct way of harvesting wild mushrooms. Only pick and eat mushrooms you have positively identified as edible, some are deadly and extreme caution is necessary (see back). Usually the season for most varieties span the autumn months, depending on the weather conditions. By cutting or pinching mushrooms off at the base of the stem without disturbing the mycelium, you allow further growth throughout their season. Some like the Hedgehog fungus, when clustered, continue to grow better if you only pick every other one. Cut or brush any dirt off mushrooms before placing them in your basket, so that no dirt falls into the gills of others in the basket. Be warned, mushroom hunting, preparing and cooking can be addictive!

'Tuber magnatum' - white truffle.   'Tuber melanosporum' - black truffle

Truffles grow in symbiosis with the roots of oak, hazel, popular or beech trees. Harvested in the winter months by specially trained pigs or dogs, which are attracted by the scent the truffle releases in the hope that it will be eaten, so that its spores will be dispersed by the animals droppings. The black truffle from Perigord is acknowledged supreme, edible raw but usually used with cooked food. They will last for two weeks if kept refrigerated in an airtight container with rice to absorb the moisture. You will also make deliciously truffle flavoured rice; the same can be done with eggs. The white truffle will only keep for a week. The best way to serve them are shaved raw with a mandoline (or a potato peeler !) over food.

'Sparassis crispa' - cauliflower fungus.

Found in coniferous woods, at tree bases. Smell is pleasant, taste sweet and nutty. Culinarily versatile, pick only when creamy-white, as when yellowing becomes tough due to age.

'Lepista saeva' - Pied bleu, Field blewit

Both this variety as well as the Wood blewit - 'Lepista nuda' have an excellent taste and smell strongly perfumed. They are extremely versatile in the kitchen, but do need cooking. The field blewit's gills are white fading with age to pale pink, the woodblewits are bluish-lilac fading to buff. Both are hardly and continue later into the winter than most mushrooms.

'Boletus edulis' - Cep or Penny bun.

Its easy of identification, delicacy of flavour and culinary versatility make this the chef's monarch of mushrooms. A chubby mushroom, the Italians call it 'porcini' meaning little pigs, and tend to grill the mature caps whole. Most chefs prefer them young when they exude little water on cooking and have a perfumed aromatic flavour. Found in grass in or near mixed woodland, pick them by twisting the stem near the base easing it away from the mycelium. By cutting them you risk leaving some of the stem to rot the mycelium stopping further growth.

'Laetiporus sulphureus' - Chicken of the woods   'Fistulina hepatica' - Ox tongue or Beefsteak fungus

Only a few of the many 'bracket' fungi, so called because of the way they grow bracketed onto trees, are edible. Fistulina hepatica - Ox tongue creates a fine colouration of the oak wood on which it grows. This 'brown oak' is much sort after by the furniture industry. Both are found in deciduous woodland, preferring oaks. They have a strong mushroomy aroma, tasting slightly sour when raw. Having a similar texture to meat, being very fleshy and succulent, sliced they can be grilled or dipped into egg yolk then breadcrumbs and fried like cutlets. The maturer specimens are good for soups or stews.

'Hydnum repandum' - Hedgehog fungus
From its appearance the French call it the 'Pied de
Mutton'. A toothed mushroom in the sense that it has tiny
white spines, hence the 'hedgehog', on its underside
instead of gills. A mild and sweet flavour similar to the
Girolle. Habitat - gregarious mainly under trees. When picking
cut every other one as they grow back better with company!

'Lentinula edodes' - Shiitake.
Found in the Far East where it has been
cultivated successfully for some time. A
strong taste, nutty and quite like a cep.
Hence chefs will often mix them with ceps
as they are less expensive. Often the stems
are tough and need to be discarded.

'Laccaria amethystea'
- Amethyst deceiver
Quite common, deep purple when moist but
drying to pale lilac buff - hence the term
'deceiver'. Needs to be cooked, taste and smell
not distinctive, somewhat holds its colour
making it attractive for decorative purposes.

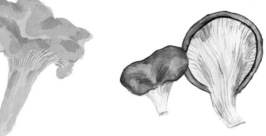

'Cantharellus { - Brown } Cantharellus
tubaeformis { Chanterelles } infundibuliformis
'Cantharellus cibarius'
- Yellow Chanterelle, Girolle "
The yellow chanterelle is by far the superior culinarily having a delicate aroma
of apricots, perfumed taste and golden trumpet like appearance. It is also called a
Girolle so it's best when talking about it to mention a colour to avoid confusion. Brown
chanterelles have a good mushroomy aroma but are not so succulent and tasty. When
picking both varieties, cut or pinch the stems and they will grow back within a few
days. Found on moist ground, often moss. Peppery taste when raw, delicious sauteed in butter.

'Pleurotus ostreatus' - Oyster mushroom
So called from their shell shape when small,
growing wild in abundance on trees, particularly rotting
ones, they are superior to the cultivated variety
having a stronger taste, although a shorter shelf life.
Culinarily very versatile, good deep fried in breadcrumbs.
When buying cultivated ones, go for the smaller
specimens as they are less watery.

'Morchella esculenta' - Morel
Belonging to the same category of fungus as the
truffle, known as the ascomycetes'. Instead of
having gills or pores the spore-bearing hymenium
lines the inside of the pits or honeycomb depressions
of the cap. Its taste and smell are pleasant and delicate
with its appearance and texture adding greatly
to its culinary attractions. Habitat - sandy soil and
burnt ground, rarely found in Britain. Good dried,
soak in hot water for 20 minutes filtering out sand.

'Craterellus cornucopioides'
- Horn of plenty.
Black trumpet like appearance,
a strong smell. With their delicate
taste and black colour they
compliment fish well. Grit often
gathers in the tubular stem, so
check when cleaning.

'Boletus badius' - Bay bolete.
Excellent tasting, a relative of the popular
'Boletus edulis' - cep, it has similar qualities.
Do not be put off by the mild blue discolouration
when it is bruised or cut. Small specimens are
delicious raw, sliced thinly in salads. Like the cep,
they soak up water if you wash them, so it is best
just to wipe them clean. Habitat - mixed woods.

assiette of venison with celeriac purée and red wine

ingredients

4 fillets of venison (not the loin)

200 g (7 oz) venison mince formed into 4 burgers

100 g (3½ oz) smoked bacon, cubed

4 medium field mushrooms, peeled and stalks removed

16 button mushrooms

16 button onions

150 g (5 oz) butter

100 ml (3 fl oz) red wine

50 ml (1½ fl oz) port

100 ml (3 fl oz) veal stock

100 ml (3 fl oz) chicken stock

150 g (5 oz) leaf spinach

For the Celeriac Purée

200 g (7 oz) celeriac

50 g (1¾ oz) butter

100 ml (3 fl oz) double cream

1 small onion

SERVES 4

Preheat the oven to 175°C/350°F/Gas Mark 4. Now make the celeriac purée. Peel the celeriac and chop into 1cm cubes. Peel and chop the onion. Melt the butter in a medium sized pan, add the onion and a good pinch of salt and sweat for two to three minutes. Add the celeriac and cook for a further 5 minutes. Cover with the cream and cook until the celeriac is soft. Purée in a food processor, set aside and keep warm.

In an ovenproof dish, melt 50 g (1¾ oz) of butter, add the lardons and fry until just golden. Add the button onions and cook until they begin to colour. Then add the chicken stock and place in the oven for 10 minutes after which the onions should be tender and the stock have reduced and glazed the onions and lardons. In a medium frying pan, melt 50g (1¾ oz) of butter. When it starts to foam, add the button mushrooms and a pinch of salt and sauté until golden. Drain the mushrooms, reserving the butter which is then returned to the pan. Add the field mushrooms and cook until they are soft. Season, drain and set aside.

Heat an ovenproof pan over a high heat. Season the venison burgers and fillets and cook on both sides to seal them. Place in the oven and roast for 2-3 minutes. Remove the venison from the pan, drain off the fat and add the port. Reduce until virtually evaporated and then add the red wine and reduce until about 1 tbsp remains. At this point add the veal stock and reduce by half. Add the button mushrooms, button onions and lardons and bring to the boil. Season and keep warm. In a large pan, melt the remaining butter and cook the spinach. Drain and keep warm.

Arrange the venison fillet and burger on two mounds of spinach on each plate and place a field mushroom on top of each burger. Spoon some purée onto each plate and pour the sauce over the venison.

 De Bortoli Shiraz Yarra Valley 1994

Saumur-Champigny Domaine du Val Brun - This Cabernet-Franc has a raspberry, fruity characteristic and comes from the Loire valley. It has a few tannis which balance out the oilinessin the pesto sauce and in the salmon.

Jacques Selosse Cuvée Exquise non vintage Sec - Created by Anselme Selosse for two of France's greatest chefs, Bernard Loiseau and Pierre Gagnaire to accompany their desserts-particularly those made with summer fruits. Made with an assemblage of somewhat younger years to retain fruitiness, acidity and freshness. With a dosage (sugar) added being somewhere between the amount for a Brut and a Demi-sec making it a Sec. Wonderful with roasted figs but also as an aperitif, when the palate demands a crisp, refreshing, slightly sweeter style.

De Bortoli Yarra Valley Shiraz 1994 Australia - This comes from the Victorian arm of the highly successful NewSouth Wales wine family. The grapes are grown at Dixons creek in the Yarra Valley producing a ripe very distinctive varietal style. 1994 was an excellent vintage producing a Shiraz with classical spicy white pepper characters and great fruit concentration. Compliments the Shiraz wine sauce with the venison well.

Pouilly-Fuissé, Château Fuissé 1995 - This Mâcon wine is vibrant with a pairing of fruit. Grown by owner Jean-Jacques Vincent who is the outstanding grower of the area. Compliments the roast cod well.

paul rankin

Paul Rankin had just come back from the States and wanted to open a 'fun' restaurant with good food, not necessarily of Michelin standard. While looking through a stack of gardening books for different vegetables to grow in his organic garden, he came across the Roscoff cauliflower. It is said that Roscoff is a Celtic name, though it is more commonly associated with a port in Northern France watched over by a lighthouse. Rankin is Irish and his cooking has a French framework; why not call his new restaurant the Roscoff Café? Friends liked the name Roscoff without

cheeses seem staple in top British restaurants. Another favourite dish is the Strangford prawns with aïoli, coriander and chilli oil – if you are ever fortunate enough to try this I guarantee it will be one of your most refreshing eating experiences. Paul is never afraid to use herbs and spices in unique and interesting ways – 'hot' food might be considered a house speciality. 'Because I was trained at Le Gavroche I use classical French methods, but because I have travelled I get excited and like to play around with the food a bit. I am still developing, still figuring out what it is I want to do.'

the 'Café', so Roscoff opened in Belfast in 1989 and became the first Michelin-starred restaurant in Northern Ireland.

At the restaurant, the philosophy is global and, with modern supply routes faster and more efficient than ever, Europe is considered 'local' as far as ingredients are concerned. Paul always chooses the best and has no doubt that fish is the strongest main local ingredient in Belfast. 'Our hake is not as trendy as tuna, but I guarantee it's better than any imported tuna from Portugal.'

His cheese board uses only Irish and British cheeses – he has never understood why French

Paul Rankin believes in food that is 'refined', not 'confined', which he thinks is often the end result at some of the more 'stuffy' establishments. He has never lost the belief that all food, no matter how developed and transformed by creative hands, must provide sustenance for the body, 'soul' as he calls it. He thinks modern cuisine should be healthy. As for the setting, he likes casual dining, a place where you can go in jeans and a T-shirt if you want and still get the same quality of service you would find in more formal operations – with the addition of that friendly Irish touch. 'I don't mean 'soul' in a spiritual sense. I cook

Roscoff's soulful kitchen   Richard Bramble 98

food that I want to eat, that is exciting to eat. A lot of people end up cooking for someone else. I think by cooking for yourself you come up with something more soulful.'

Besides cooking, Paul and his wife, Jeanne, like to travel – indeed, they met each other while travelling, and distant lands have provided the inspiration for many of their dishes. When I met him he told me about the time his restlessness began. Paul Rankin grew up in Ballywalter, a seaside village in County Down, until the family moved to Belfast in 1969. Deeply religious at the time, Paul was already planning to be a missionary or a preacher when still in his teens at the Royal Belfast Academical Institution, a boys' public school in the city where rugby was his main distraction from the Scriptures. Eventually, the conventional religious path seemed too constricting for his inquiring mind and he

went to Queen's University to read biochemistry. But he still had not found what he was looking for and dropped out to hitch-hike round Europe. He returned and tried one last time to make his parents happy by enrolling at the British School of Osteopathy in London – four months later he was backpacking his way to the eastern Mediterranean.

Jeanne is an American who grew up in Winnipeg, Canada. In 1980 she was working as a ship's cook in Greece. Paul was working as a boat painter in a marina just outside Athens when they both met. He says that she seduced him and they fell in love sailing round the ancient Aegean islands. Jeanne took Paul to Canada for 18 months where they both worked the Vancouver restaurant scene to save up their money to go travelling again. Even as a waiter Paul knew this was the business for him and he started to become interested in every small detail of the food preparation.

1982 saw the couple in Sri Lanka, then on to India and beyond, visiting Goa, Delhi, Nepal, Himachal Pradesh and Kashmir; the exotic foods they experienced led to their deciding how they wanted to cook for themselves. It was not, however, until they were in Australia that they received advice to return to Europe to work in a 'serious' kitchen before they were too old. Paul was given an introduction to Albert Roux and offered a job. He decided to delay it a year and discover the food of Malaysia, Thailand and China with Jeanne.

At the start of 1984, Paul arrived in London to wash dishes at Le Gavroche. Jeanne followed suit and got a job in the pastry section of the Roux brothers' City outlet, Le Poulbot. A few months later Paul and Jeanne got married. They stayed with the Rouxs for just over two years with Paul, a 'green and naive mature student', continually teased that, at twenty-four, he was too old to learn how to cook. He had the last laugh and is convinced that his maturity enabled him to learn four or five times as much as the usual teenage commis

chefs learn in their training periods. In 1986, Paul and Jeanne returned to Canada, where their first daughter, Claire, was born. It looked as if things were looking up for the Rankins when Paul landed the role of executive chef at an experimental hotel and restaurant in the Napa Valley, California, but the rogue employer failed to pay and they ended up in the red with Jeanne six months pregnant with their second child, Emily.

True to the Bob Marley song, another door opens when one door closes; Paul was persuaded by his brothers to return to Belfast to open a restaurant on the site of a bankrupt Indian restaurant. Paul remembers it being the curry house version of the Marie Celeste, the kitchen left as if the chefs had suddenly abandoned it in the middle of cooking, the smell of curry still pervading the air. After a lot of time and effort, it looked as if the site might be cursed as their new restaurant faced the possibility of the receivers as well. Ironically, they were saved by the one thing they were not aiming for – a Michelin star. When the local papers broke the news of Roscoff's success in gaining the accolade, the road to solvency was

being on your feet sixteen hours a day. Maybe I just need to recharge my batteries properly.'

Perhaps he was thinking of Jeanne who had just had their third child and was taking a year off – Jeanne has spent her catering career getting into the kitchen at four in the morning to bake the breads and head the pastry sections. At the restaurant it is very much a two-man band, and Jeanne is still doing the paperwork and writing the pastry recipes at home. Paul tries to make time for himself and his family and likes to walk for an hour every morning in the riverside park area. He practises yoga and finds that this helps him to cope with the stress of the restaurant trade. But there is a lot of pressure, with TV and writing now adding to his duties as a master chef with a business that is booming. Roscoff won the BBC's Good Food Guide Award for 1996/7 which Paul appreciated because he sometimes feels detached from the British scene, the restaurant perhaps not getting the attention it deserves. As well as the restaurant they have one café in Belfast close to City Hall, Donegall Square, with more to follow. Paul foresees a growing market. 'At the top end there is a good choice of exclusive restaurants; at the lower end pubs are improving all the time. There is a lot of scope in the middle.'

Paul drove me to Fountain Street in his Mercedes sports car and told me that the café is managed by Gillian Hayes, who has been at Roscoff right from the start. The café speciality is its continental-style breads, though the Irish traditional 'wheaten' is the most popular, and the in-house bakery supplies other cafés and outlets, including

suddenly clear. More importantly for Paul and Jeanne, they had been awarded the star for food that had been created on their terms, food they would want to eat.

After the star they kept the prices as low as they could to keep the volume of customers up – they wanted to retain the lively atmosphere. They played jazz music at Roscoff: Paul's brother-in-law, Mark Lebrun, is a jazz musician and they once teamed up with him to produce a book and CD combination called *Hot Food, Cool Jazz* – an edition of 8,000 sold out in the space of a few months. Of course, all this atmosphere inevitably means lots of meals, which means lots of work in the kitchen. Paul told me he was feeling his age. 'Once you reach thirty the physical job of cooking takes its toll. You find it hard to recover from constantly

Tesco. The other thing not to miss is the coffee. When I was painting a picture outside the café, two people came up and asked me what coffee the café uses as it was superb and they wanted to buy it; the staff would not tell them. 'If you're in the know,' they said, 'mention the brand in your book and we'll buy it.'

Paul's cooking is constantly evolving with strong influences of asian and ethnic cuisine. In 2000 it therefore seemed appropriate on a refurbishment of the restaurant to rename it 'Cayenne', the name of a spice, to reflect this. Perhaps this fresh image is indicative of Northern Ireland in general with most people looking forward to a new era of optimism, albeit with a little more grass roots realism than the platitudinous politicians. Roscoff experienced the troubles first-hand when a bomb went off in a taxi. Pieces of the vehicle ended up in the back of the restaurant. The next evening they hosted an Italian wine evening as if nothing had happened. Paul remembers one of the Italian wine-makers being ushered past the neatly swept glass, not quite knowing what it was as it looked like piles of snow.

Although the restaurant business is relatively challenging in its call upon you to change and adapt to circumstances, Paul will never allow himself to fall into a rut and constantly questions his life at every stage, not wanting to tie himself down by habit. 'Just because I am a chef now doesn't mean I am always going to be a chef. It's nice to develop, to let yourself grow as you get old. Roscoff developed into Cayenne. I still think about travelling a lot. Every chef should take time off to cook in

other countries. For example, cooking in India, the flavours are so fascinating, so delicious when cooked from scratch with fresh herbs.'

I left him with his dreams of Jeanne and himself and his young family in faraway places. As I boarded my airplane back to the mainland, I was already looking forward to the next time I would be in Northern Ireland and could once more enjoy the food of Paul Rankin.

'Coriandrum sativum

Coriander is part of the same family as the carrot and is a native of
southern Europe, North Africa and the Middle East. It gets its name from
'koris', a Greek word meaning 'bug' because it's green leaves are said to
have a smell reminiscent of the smell of bed bugs. It is an annual that
ought to be grown from seed in spring in an open, sunny situation. It prefers
a warm, light, dry soil and flourishes beside chervil and dill. It germinates
quickly and you ought to have some leaves to use within five weeks.
Harvest the seeds in late summer and lay them to dry in a warm place for
a few days before storing in airtight jars.
    Fresh coriander leaves can be used as a garnish in a similar way to parsley,
but more sparingly if using them chopped. They are delicious with spicy
dishes of the Middle East and are extensively used in Latin-American
cooking. It is, however, the dried seeds that are used most frequently,
essential ingredients in most Indian curry dishes and in the spice mixture
known as 'garam masala'. Coriander seeds are combined with
juniper to give flavour to gin. The root is used a flavour unique to
Thai cooking.
    It was one of the few medicinal plants listed on the 8th century Babylonian
clay tablets. Roman legions used to carry the seeds to flavour bread on
their travels and brought the herb to Britain.

fishcakes with aïoli and coriander

ingredients

250 g (9 oz) hake fillet, skinned

250 g (9 oz) salmon fillet, skinned

4 tbsp butter

2 shallots, finely chopped

½ glass dry white wine

250 g (9 oz) mashed potatoes, cooled

4 tbsp snipped chives

2 tbsp chopped coriander

1 tbsp Dijon mustard

salt and cayenne pepper

flour, eggwash and breadcrumbs

2 tbsp light olive oil

For the Aïoli

½ bunch coriander leaves, roughly chopped

2 egg yolks

2 garlic cloves, finely sliced

2 tsp lemon juice

¼ tsp salt

125 ml (4 fl oz) light olive oil

125 ml (4 fl oz) vegetable oil

SERVES 6

Check the fish for bones and then dice into pieces of approximately 2.5cm. Melt 2 tbsp of butter in a small pan and sweat off the shallots for 2 minutes. Add the wine and the fish, season lightly with salt and cover with a tight lid. Cook gently for 4-5 minutes until the fish is just cooked. Drain any juice from the fish and allow to cool.

While the fish is cooling, prepare the aioli. Combine the coriander, egg yolks, garlic, lemon juice and salt in a food processor. Blend for a few seconds and then slowly add the oils in a steady stream until the mixture has emulsified. Set aside.

Next, take the cooled fish and flake it roughly. Mix it gently with the mashed potato, herbs, mustard and a little salt and cayenne pepper. Divide the mix into 12 balls, then, with a light dusting of flour, form the balls into little patties, brush them with the eggwash and coat lightly with breadcrumbs.

Heat the remaining butter with the light olive oil in a large frying pan over a high heat. Sauté the cakes for 2-3 minutes on each side. Drain on paper towels. Serve with a little aïoli, and a garnish of diced and sautéed red and yellow peppers, and rocket leaves.

 Riesling, 2nd Humbrecht, Alsace 1996

risotto cakes with prawns

ingredients

16-20 cooked prawn tails

2 tbsp vegetable oil

2 tbsp butter

For the Risotto Cakes

30 g (1 oz) butter

1 shallot finely chopped

150 g (5 oz) arborio rice

600 ml (1 pt) fish stock

salt and freshly ground white pepper

2 tbsp chopped parsley

2 tbsp chopped basil

50 g (2 oz) flour

2 tbsp butter

For the Tomato Sauce

2 tbsp light vegetable oil

1 shallot, chopped

2 cloves garlic, chopped

1 small red chilli, de-seeded and chopped

2 tsp of tomato paste

2 tsp anchovy fillet, chopped

1 kg (2 lb 4 oz) tomatoes

3 tbsp extra virgin olive oil

3 tbsp chopped basil

SERVES 4

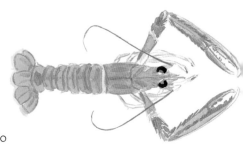

First prepare the risotto. Melt the butter in a heavy based pan and fry the shallot until soft and transparent. Add the arborio rice and stir well so that all the grains are coated with the butter. After about 2 minutes, slowly start adding the fish stock, a ladleful at a time. When the rice is cooked, season to taste and add the parsley and basil. Turn out onto a baking tray and allow to cool. Once it is cool, take a small handful, roll it into a ball and coat it lightly in flour. Flatten it into a small pattie, about 1cm thick and 3-4 cm wide. Make two patties for each person. Heat a heavy based frying pan over a medium-high heat and add 2 tbsp of butter. Fry the risotto cakes until they are golden brown and crispy, and keep them warm in a low oven.

Next, prepare the tomato sauce. Peel and chop the tomatoes. Heat the vegetable oil in a pan and sweat off the shallot, garlic and chilli. When the shallot is soft, add first the tomato paste, then the anchovy. Pour in the roughly chopped tomatoes and simmer for 5-8 minutes, until the tomatoes have collapsed and everything is heated through. Just before serving, add the extra virgin olive oil and the basil.

Remove the prawns from their shells. Heat a heavy based frying pan over a high heat and add 2 tbsp of oil and 2 tbsp of butter. Sauté the prawns until they are lightly browned and heated through - this should only take a few minutes.

Place 2 risotto cakes in the centre of each warmed plate and spoon over some of the sauce. Arrange the prawn tails around and on top and then spoon some more of the sauce aroud the plate. Garnish with herbs and serve immediately.

 Chardonnay Greenpoint, Yarra Valley, Australia 1995

confit of rabbit leg and a saffron barley risotto

ingredients

4 rabbit legs, thigh bones removed

2 tsp fine salt

1 tsp cracked black pepper

2 cloves of garlic, roughly chopped

1 bay leaf

1 x 750g jar or tin of duck fat

For the Sauce

250 ml (8 fl oz) rich brown chicken stock

6 plum tomatoes, peeled, de-seeded and quartered

8 leaves of fresh basil, cut into fine strips

1 tsp butter

salt and freshly ground black pepper

For the Barley Risotto

150 g (5 oz) barley

50 g (1¾ oz) butter

40 g (1½ oz) carrots, finely sliced

40 g (1½ oz) celery, finely sliced

salt and freshly ground black pepper

pinch of saffron threads

1 litre (1 pt 13 fl oz) hot chicken stock

50 ml (1½ fl oz) double cream

SERVES 4

Lay the rabbit in a deep plate and season evenly with the salt, pepper, garlic and herbs. Cover and leave in the fridge overnight.

Remove from the fridge and wipe off the seasoning, then place in a casserole with the melted duck fat. Bring to the boil and then simmer gently for about 1 hour. Allow to cool in the fat.

Next, make the risotto. Rinse the barley well and drain. Melt 15 g (½ oz) of the butter in a pan, add the vegetables and a little salt and sweat them gently for 3-4 minutes until soft. Add the saffron and barley and continue to cook for 1 minute.

Pour in enough of the hot chicken stock to cover the barley and simmer gently. Cook uncovered 20-25 minutes, stirring every couple of minutes until the barley is cooked. As the liquid is absorbed, add more of the hot stock. To finish, add the double cream and stir in the remaining butter.

To pepare the sauce, reduce the brown chicken stock until it is slightly syrupy, then add the tomato quarters and a little salt and pepper. Warm the tomatoes in the sauce until they soften, and then stir in the butter and basil. While the sauce is cooking, warm the rabbit legs gently in the fat, then, if desired, brown them off in a hot pan or under the grill.

To serve, spoon the barley risotto into 4 bowls, place the confit legs on top and surround with the sauce and tomatoes.

 Barbera D'Asti 'Valle del Sole' Michaele Chiarlo, Italy 1994

roast fillet of monkfish with mediterranean vegetables and anchovy butter

4 x 225 g (8 oz) monkfish fillets

salt and white pepper

1 tbsp light olive oil

1 tbsp butter

1 courgette, sliced and sautéed

2 Asian aubergines, sliced and sautéed

1 red pepper, roasted, peeled and sliced

8 new potatoes, cooked and sliced

For the Anchovy Butter

150 ml (5 fl oz) dry white wine

2 heaped tbsp chopped shallots

½ tspn garlic, finely chopped

1 tbsp parsley, chopped

1 tsp fresh thyme, chopped

1 tsp fresh rosemary, chopped

10 anchovy fillets, minced

125 g (4 oz) soft butter

SERVES 4

Trim any dark flesh from the monkfish fillets and cut into four equal portions. Cut each fillet almost through horizontally then, opening it up like a book, press it gently with the heel of your hand to flatten. Set aside.

Next, make the anchovy butter. Boil the wine with the shallots in a small pan over a medium high heat. Reduce the wine by half, allow to cool and then whisk into the butter with the other ingredients. Set aside.

Season the monkfish with the salt and pepper. Heat a large frying pan over a moderately high heat. Add the butter and oil and, when the butter starts to foam, add the monkfish fillets. Fry for about 5 minutes, then turn them over carefully and cook for another 3 minutes.

Arrange the Mediterranean vegetables onto warmed plates, place the monkfish in the middle and top with a spoonful of anchovy butter.

 Fleurie 'Château du Fleurie', Loron et Fils, Beaujolais 1996

white chocolate cheesecake with a blueberry compote

ingredients

For the Base

70 g (2½ oz) digestive biscuits

35 g (1¼ oz) toasted ground almonds

50 g (1¾ oz) caster sugar

1 tsp lemon zest

40 g (1½ oz) unsalted butter, melted

For the Filling

1 kg (2 lb 3 oz) cream cheese

4 eggs

500 g (1 lb 2 oz) white chocolate, melted

2 tbsp Amaretto liqueur

1 tbsp vanilla extract

For the Almond Praline

150 g (5½ oz) toasted almonds

150 g (5½ oz) caster sugar

2 tbsp water

2 tsp vegetable oil

For the Blueberry Compote

450 g (1 lb) blueberries

juice of a lemon

200 g (7 oz) caster sugar

SERVES 12

First prepare the almond praline. Put the sugar and water in a small pan and place over a medium high heat. When it has coloured to a medium golden, add the toasted almonds and swirl to coat evenly. Grease a baking sheet with the vegetable oil and turn the almond and caramel mixture out onto it. Leave to cool. Once cool, pulse in a food processor to grind to a fairly fine consistency. Next, to make the base of the cheesecake, mix all the ingredients in a small bowl. The texture should be rather moist. Grease a 9" springform tin well, and press the base into the bottom of the tin, to a thickness of about ½ cm.

Place the cream cheese in a food processor and mix until it is softened. Add the eggs, Amaretto and vanilla extract and pulse again. When smooth, add the melted, but not hot, chocolate. Blend until smooth. Transfer to a bowl and fold in 2 or 3 handfuls of the praline. Pour the filling carefully into the prepared tin, to approximately ⅞ full. Bake in a slow oven (150°C/300°F Gas Mark 2) for about 1 hour. The centre of the cheesecake should still be slightly wobbly after this time, but it will firm up as it cools.

While the cheesecake is baking, make the blueberry compote. Place the blueberries and sugar in a small pan and heat gently. The berries will release some liquid which, depending on the amount, may need to be reduced slightly. If so, simply simmer until the juice reaches the desired consistency. Remove from the heat, add lemon juice to taste and allow to cool. To serve, set slices of the cheesecake on each plate and surround with some of the compote. A sprinkle of the praline makes a pretty garnish for the plate.

 Black Muscat 'Elysium' Andrew Quady, California 1996

tangy lemon pudding with strawberries

ingredients

4 eggs, separated

75 ml (2½ fl oz) lemon juice

2 tsp lemon zest

1 tbsp unsalted butter, melted

300 g (10½ oz) caster sugar

100 g (3½ oz) plain flour

½ tsp salt

375 ml (12½ fl oz) milk

450 g (1 lb) strawberries

strawberry coulis (see below)

mint sprigs, to garnish

creme fraiche to garnish

For the Tangy Sauce

50 ml (1¾ fl oz) golden syrup

1 tsp lemon zest

75 ml (2½ fl oz) fresh lemon juice

50 g (1¾ oz) icing sugar, sifted

For the Strawberry Coulis

250 g (9 oz) strawberries

1 tbsp lemon juice

100 g (3½ oz) icing sugar, sifted

SERVES 6-8

Pre-heat the oven to 175°C/350°F/Gas Mark 4 and get a roasting tin ready to be used as a bain-marie for baking the puddings.

Prepare the strawberry coulis by blending the ingredients together in a blender. Taste for sweetness and add more sugar or lemon as required. Strain through a sieve and refrigerate until needed.

In a mixer, cream together the egg yolks, lemon juice, lemon zest and melted butter until thick, and light in colour. Next, sift together 200 g (7 oz) of the sugar, the flour and the salt. With the mixer on low speed, alternately add the sifted dry ingredients and the milk, starting and ending with the dry ingredients.

In another bowl, whisk the egg white to soft peaks and, while still whisking, slowly add the remaining 100 g (3½ oz) of sugar. When the whites are stiff and glossy, fold them into the mixture. Spoon the pudding batter into greased moulds to approximately full. Place the moulds in the roasting tin, fill with hot water to halfway up the sides of the moulds and bake for 30-40 minutes. While the puddings are baking, place all of the ingredients for the sauce in a small pan and bring to the boil over a medium heat. Simmer for 2 minutes then remove from the heat.

When the puddings are ready, allow them to cool slightly, then transfer them carefully to dessert plates. Surround with the tangy lemon sauce, fresh strawberries and a drizzle of strawberry coulis and garnish with mint and, if desired, creme fraiche.

 Château La Rame, St-Croix-du-Mont, Bordeaux 1995

rose gray & ruth rogers

I am always at home at The River Cafe, as it feels like a gallery or artist's studio, where masters and students are rapturously caught in concentrated creativity and the audience, the diners, are privileged in attending the private view. Rose Gray attended Guildford Art School in the late fifties, then taught art at Shoreditch Comprehensive. Indeed, culture seems to surround Rose wherever she is. She once lived in a flat which formed part of a large period house in Hampstead and, in lieu of rent, used to cook for the owners, a graphic designer Henri Henrion and his sculptor wife Daphne. In 1961 she married Michael Gray, a film editor, and they had three children: Hester, Ossie and Lucy. Eight years later Rose and Michael parted and she met David MacIlwaine, an artist and sculptor. Rose and David have a son called Dante. It was at the art school in Guildford that Rose met the architect, Richard Rogers, and his Italian mother, Dada, a phenomenal guiding force in the kitchen. In 1981 Rose and David moved to Tuscany and Rose immersed herself in the cooking of the region.

Ossie joined the family to spend a year there after school and fondly remembers Rose researching a book on pasta and trying all the recipes out on them. Rose was destined to meet Ruth Rogers, or 'Ruthie' as she is known, when Ruthie married Richard in 1973. Ruthie, from upstate New York, came to London in 1967 and had no choice in learning to become a great cook with Dada for a mother-in-law. I met Ruth Rogers in 1995 and was enthusiastic about The River Cafe as it basked in the sunshine on the edge of the Thames. Pumpkins, like the fat cheeks of a smiling clown, bulged from large boxes resting on the lawn. On the wall aubergines, tomatoes and peppers were ripening – as far as I know, in no other restaurant in London will you find this. At the time I was rather shy, as I was just starting to learn the culinary ropes of the industry, so I did not dare venture into the kitchen. Three years and many restaurants later, I now dive into a kitchen at the first bang of a pot, and The River Cafe kitchen is one of my favourites. One of the first times I met Rose Gray she had been working on her new vegetable boxes and had just pruned a tree. She had an odd request for me before we started talking about cooking. 'It looks bare, Richard, ' she said, looking at the tree. 'Would you mind blending in the pruning scars with your watercolours?'

As I speak, The River Cafe has a Michelin star, but Rose and Ruth do not entirely agree with the Michelin food ethic. Their concern is that the Michelin identity attracts the customer who expects a certain 'type' of food and service. They see their restaurant as a place to relax, to enjoy friendly intelligent service and to eat delicious food, undisguised by sauces in the Italian way.

Rose and Ruth are supported in the kitchen by their charming head chef, Theo. But over the

years a number of young chefs have come through the doors of the Rivercafe and been influenced by Rose and Ruth's style of cooking. Many have gone on to open their own restaurants and become well known in their own right. In 1995 the young and unknown Jamie Oliver, remembers curiously watching me from the kitchen window whilst cooking as I painted a watercolour of the outside. Indeed it was here that Jamie Oliver learnt many of his culinary skills. Both Jamie Oliver and Hugh Fearnley Whittington, who has also worked at The Rivercafe, have gone on to have successful television series.

Ossie, not wanting to work directly for his mother, is self-employed as the general manager and has developed and nurtured the all-Italian wine list. Previously, he worked for Bibendum Wines and took on the role as general manager in 1994. Ossie is someone who likes to rock the boat whenever he can, not because he is disruptive, but because he has a natural curiosity to see what happens when he tries

something new. Most people say that a wine cannot be effectively matched with a chocolate dish, especially the famed chocolate nemesis, but Ossie manages it with a Bellavista Franciacorta, an Italian equivalent to an excellent Champagne. Chocolate nemesis is the most popular dessert on their menu, and I really enjoy making it at home.

Another time I met Rose, it was during a lunch service. She had not had breakfast so she was having a seagull's egg with a bit of chilli. That day they were serving as a starter boiled sea gull's egg with parmesan and asparagus. Rose explained that the sea gull's egg is quite special – lovely and rich – as you can only get them in the month of May when people are allowed to collect them. The fixed element in The River Cafe's cooking is its respect for the seasons and for the freshest possible ingredients of each season. Rose and Ruthie sit with their chefs every day and put together the menu, discussing what ingredients are particularly good. The variable element is the menu's creativity which sees lots of improvisation and change every service which, in turn, encourages more creativity and interest in the cooking from the chefs. I once watched, fascinated, as Rose put together a turbot dish slightly differently three times in one service. In effect, the diner is getting an original work every time. Rose, a grandmother, looks much younger than her years when she works, especially when she is in the kitchen: perhaps Picasso and Matisse, who kept their youthful energies until they died, appeared similarly. I like to think that people are kept young by being completely sincere and honest through love, and I sympathise with Matisse: 'Is not love the origin of all creation?'

Ingredients are paramount to Rose and Ruth and, with their natural gift of flavour detection, nothing but the best can get past them – they have been known to chase down the road after a delivery van if sub-standard produce has been left. The River Cafe likes to use organic suppliers as often as possible. Adrian Barren lives at Brentleigh Hall in Suffolk where there is an eighteenth century walled garden. This, combined with the Suffolk climate, creates a perfect environment to grow many unusual Italian and English vegetables. He even uses the surplus to rear pigs, which he supplies to the River Cafe. One of the first organic farms, Sunnyfields, owned by a friend of Rose, started back in 1988 to grow black cabbages from seeds that Rose and Ruth had brought back from Italy. Often they will pick vegetables at five o'clock, and deliver them to the River Cafe for service at eight. The Thames Wharf kitchen uses many unusual vegetable varieties, not least a white aubergine from Italy, which has a whiter flesh, fewer seeds and is sweeter than the purple variety. As for the Capri lemons they use, they are probably the best anywhere in the world and a large segment comes with all grilled meat and fish dishes.

The heart of the kitchen, reminiscent of an earlier, more romantic period, is the Italian wood-burning oven which Rose first used during the seventies and which, when roasting at temperatures as high as 600°C, seals things quickly, keeps in the moisture, intensifies the flavours and makes for more succulence. Turbot steaks take six minutes instead of the usual twenty in 350°C ovens. When cooling down, the oven can produce the most succulent overnight roasts like suckling pig. Outside of service the less hot oven is used to roast vegetables and fruit, or bake a lemon tart; nectarines can be roasted with vanilla sugar and served with Italian brandy. Rose and David first discovered

they have been carefully preparing for the customers. Another habit unique to the restaurant is the waiting staff helping the cooks prepare all the herbs and vegetables in the morning, before changing into service togs to go out on to the dining room floor – this way they really get to know the ingredients and have a feel for the food they serve. Rose and Ruth are more sensitive than most chef patrons and fifty per cent of the staff are women – this makes for a very pleasant working environment without too many egos bouncing off one another. Every year they make a trip with a few of the chefs, wine staff and managers to meet the wine producers and to taste the vintage and the new season of olive oil. Everyone will, at some point, go wine tasting and get to know most of the wine producers. One chef told me that every top kitchen should be run like this, believing that if a kitchen is friendly then this transfers to the food. Perhaps this is why everything seems that touch more beautiful at The River Cafe: the diners, relieved of tension and softer because of it; the staff, in their whites appearing as angels when reflected in the frosted glass panels behind the bar. From the artist's and the epicure's point of view there are so many natural compositions.

wood-burning stoves when they bought and sold antique ones in the early seventies.

Overall, the restaurant and kitchen has an atmosphere, for both diners and staff, that can best be described as loving. People like working here because they are treated well; there is not the old-fashioned distinction between customer and worker in which the worker is treated like dirt and given the minimum to keep him or her going like a slave. For example, the staff sit down after the lunch and dinner services to enjoy the food that

"Menu Meeting"

149

grilled squid with chillies

SERVES 6

6 hand-sized squid

12 large red chillies, de-seeded and very finely chopped

sea salt and pepper

8 tbsp oil and lemon dressing

225 g (8 oz) rocket leaves

3 lemons

extra olive oil

Prepare each squid for cleaning by cutting open the body to make one flat piece, keeping the tentacles in their bunches. Scrape out the guts, remove the eyes and mouth and wash. Use a serated knife to score the inner side of the body with criss-crossing parallel lines about 1 cm apart. Make the sauce by tossing the chilli into a bowl, covering with an inch of oil and seasoning with salt and pepper. Place each full squid under a very hot grill, scored side down, for 1-2 minutes; turn over and cook until the flesh curls up. Toss the rocket in the oil and lemon dressing. Arrange the six squid bodies and their tentacles on individual plates with some of the rocket. Place a little chilli on each squid and serve with lemon quarters.

 Soave Classico 1996 Pieropan

zucchini soup

ingredients

1 kg (2 lb 4 oz) trimmed medium zucchini

25 ml (1 fl oz) olive oil

2 garlic cloves, peeled and chopped

sea salt and pepper

500 ml (17 fl oz) chicken stock or water

140 ml (4 fl oz) double cream

1 small bunch basil, chopped

1 small bunch flat-leaf parsley, chopped

120 g (4 oz) freshly grated parmesan

6 slices ciabatta bread

115 g (4 oz) stoned and chopped black olives

1 large red chilli, de-seeded

extra virgin olive oil

SERVES 6

Cut the zucchini lengthwise into quarters, then into 2.5 cm (1 in) pieces. Heat the oil in a heavy saucepan and cook the garlic and zucchini slowly for approximately 25 minutes until the zucchini are brown and very soft. Add salt, pepper and the stock, and simmer for another few minutes. Remove from the stove.

Put three-quarters of the zucchini in a food processor and purée. Return to the pan and add the cream, basil, parsley and parmesan.

To make the crostini, toast the bread on both sides. Mix the olives and chilli with some extra virgin olive oil and spread thickly on the crostini. Serve at the side of the plate.

 Chianti Rufina 1996, Fattoria Selvapiana

wood-roasted turbot tranche with capers

ingredients

6 x 225 g (8 oz) slices turbot on the bone

2 tbsp olive oil

salt and pepper

juice of 3 lemons

1 sliced lemon

6 tbsp chopped celery leaves

6 tbsp chopped flat-leaf parsley

12 tbsp salted capers

FOR 6

Preheat the oven to 230°C/450°F/Gas Mark 8. Take the turbot slices, lightly brush with olive oil and season with salt and pepper. Place side by side on a flat baking tray and bake for 15-20 minutes, depending on size. When done, transfer the fish to 4 separate serving plates. Add the lemon juice, celery leaves, half the parsley and the capers to the baking tray and heat for a minute or so over a hot flame so that the ingredients combine with the fish juices. Pour over the individual turbot slices, sprinkle with parsely and serve with a slice of lemon.

 Valpolicella Classico Allegrini 'La Griola' 1994

marinated grilled lamb

ingredients

2.25 kg (5 lb) leg spring lamb, boned and butterflied

5 cloves garlic, crushed

2 tbsp rosemary, chopped

pinch coarse black pepper

2 tbsp lemon juice

3 tbsp olive oil

1 tbsp sea salt

SERVES 6

Mix the crushed garlic, rosemary and pepper in a bowl. Rub it into the cut side of the meat. Place the meat in a shallow dish and pour over the lemon juice and olive oil. Turn the meat over a couple of times to make sure it is coated, then cover. Leave to marinate at room temperature overnight or for at least 4 hours, turning the meat occasionally.

Preheat a grill to a very high temperature. Remove the meat from the marinade and pat dry. Season with salt. Carefully place the meat on the grill and seal on both sides. Lower the heat and continue to grill until the desired degree of pinkness, turning once. Allow at least 8 minutes per side.

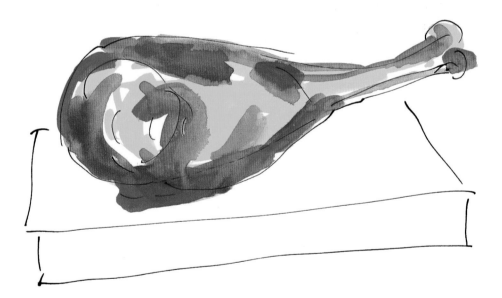

 Pinot Vero 1996, Franz Haas, Montagna, Alto Adige

baked fresh borlotti beans

2 kg (4½ lb) fresh borlotti beans, podded

3 large tomatoes

1 whole garlic clove with skin

1 bunch fresh sage

120 ml (4 fl oz) extra virgin olive oil

salt and freshly ground black pepper

SERVES 6

Preheat the oven to 200°C/400°F/Gas Mark 6. Choose a saucepan or casserole that you can put in your oven. The size of the pan is important: the beans should fill it to halfway up the sides. Put in the beans, whole tomatoes, garlic and sage, and pour in cold water just to come within 5 mm (¼ in) of the top of the beans. Pour in the olive oil, and make a hole in the middle with the point of a knife to allow steam to escape.

Place the beans in a preheated oven and bake for three quarters to one hour. The water evaporates during cooking, and the beans will soak up the olive oil, becoming creamy and soft. Season generously with salt and pepper. Serve with a little extra olive oil.

This is the modern way of cooking borlotti beans. The old way was to use a wide-style chianti bottle stripped of its straw cradle. The beans were placed inside with water and olive oil, and hay was stuffed in the neck to make sure the water was absorbed rather than evaporated.

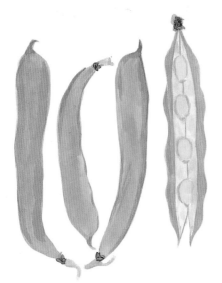

Broad beans are native to the Mediterranean basin, seeds have been found in Egypt dating back 2400 BC. The Greeks and Romans thought highly of them, and they were the staple food in the Middle Ages. It is the hardiest of beans and the only one which will survive the winter frosts so it can be harvested in early summer. In parts of Italy "Fava" is eaten raw, young in the pods with pecorino cheese. Fresh beans are delicious cooked with mint and mashed with olive oil. Dried ones are good for soups, soak as for borlotti beans.

Borlotti beans have an appearance that gives them the name "fagioli scritti" – written beans. Avaliable fresh in August and September, they are usually purchased dry. Borlotti di Lamon are the largest, most superior and most expensive. If dried, soak overnight in a cold bowl of water with two tablespoons of bicarbonate of soda to soften the skins.

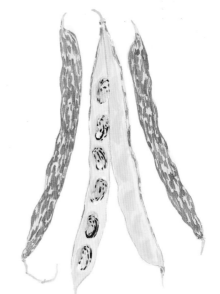

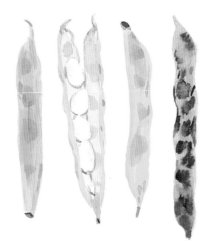

Cannellini beans have a nutty taste, creamy texture and are avaliable fresh in July and August. The pods may be discoloured with mildrew but the beans are normally fine inside. The beans will take up flavours of strong herbs so cook gently without strong seasonings, fresh sage, tomato and garlic in the cooking water is good. Make sure the dried ones are not too old as they will have tough skins, and soak as for borlotti beans.

pan roasted guinea fowl stuffed with sage, prosciutto, marsala and lemon

ingredients

2 x 3 lb guinea fowl, boned

1 whole lemon

1 bunch sage leaves

2 cloves garlic

225g (8 oz) prosciutto, fat retained

sea salt

coarsely ground pepper

1 large glass dry marsala

900 g (2 lb) swiss chard, washed, with thick stalks removed

1 clove garlic, sliced

1 small dried red chilli

2 tbsp olive oil

SERVES 4

Chop the lemon and prosciutto roughly. Place the sage, lemon pieces, prosciutto with the garlic in a food processor, and pulse to a coarse texture. Remove mixture and season generously.

Loosen the guinea fowl's skin, and push a tablespoon of the mixture into the cavity.

Place the guinea fowl on a large flat tray. Season generously and leave to marinate for 30 minutes.

Preheat oven to 230°C/450°F/ Gas Mark 8. Heat the oil in an ovenproof dish. Brown the guinea fowl on each side and put into a preheated oven skin side up. Roast in the hot oven for 15-20 minutes. When cooked, the juices should run clear.

Remove the guinea fowl from the pan. Add the marsala and heat over a flame, stirring to reduce to a thick sauce. Season and pour over the guinea fowl.

Blanch the chard in a large pan of boiling water with plenty of salt, until al dente. Drain and dry.

Heat the oil in a large flat pan. Add sliced garlic and dried red chilli. Brown the garlic and add blanched chard. Turn chard briefly in the spicy flavoured oil for 2-3 minutes.

 Chianti Classico 1996, Isole e Olena

chocolate nemesis

ingredients

675 g (1 lb) bitter sweet chocolate, broken into small pieces

10 eggs

575 g (1 lb 5 oz) caster sugar

450 g (1 lb) soft unsalted butter

Preheat the oven to 160°C/325°F/Gas Mark 3. Line a 30 × 5 cm (12 × 2 in) cake tin with greaseproof paper, then grease and flour it.

Beat the eggs with a third of the sugar until the volume quadruples. This will take at least 10 minutes in an electric mixer.

Heat the remaining sugar in a small pan with 250 ml (8 fl oz) water until the sugar has completely dissolved to a syrup.

Place the chocolate and butter in the hot syrup and stir to combine. Remove from heat and allow to cool slightly.

Add the warm syrup to the eggs and continue to beat gently until completely combined – about 20 seconds, no more. Pour into cake tin and place in a bain-maire of hot water. It is essential if the cake is to cook evenly, that the cake tin is immersed to its brim. Bake in the oven for 30 minutes or until set. Test by placing the flat of your hand gently on the surface.

Leave to cool in the tin before turning out.

 Metodo Franciacorta Cuvée Brut NV, Bellavista

157

lemon tart

SERVES 10-12

ingredients

finely grated zest and juice of 7 lemons

350 g (12 oz) caster sugar

6 whole eggs

9 egg yolks

300 g (10 oz) soft unsalted butter

For the Sweet Pastry

350 g (12 oz) plain flour

a pinch of salt

175 g (8 oz) unsalted cold butter, cut into cubes

100 g (4 oz) icing sugar

3 egg yolks

Preheat the oven to 160°C/325°F/Gas Mark 4. Make the sweet pastry by pulsing the flour, salt and butter in a food processor until the mixture resembles coarse bread crumbs. Add the sugar then the egg yolks and pulse. The mixture will immediately combine and leave the sides of the bowl. Press the pastry into a flan tin and bake blind.

While the pastry is left to cool make the filling by putting all the ingredients except the butter in a large saucepan on a very low heat and whisk until the eggs have broken up and the sugar has dissolved.

Add half the butter and continue to whisk. At this point the eggs will start to cook and the mixture will coat the back of a spoon. Add the remaining butter and continue stirring until the mixture becomes very thick. It is important to continue whisking throughout the cooking process to prevent the mixture from curdling. Remove from the heat, place on a cold surface and continue to whisk until lukewarm.

Raise the oven temperature to 230°C/450°F/Gas Mark 8. Spoon the lemon filling into the pastry base and bake until the top is brown. This should take about 5-8 minutes.

 Recioto di Soave 'Le Colombare' 1995 Pieropan

Soave Classico 1996, Pieropan, Soave, Veneto – Leonildo Pieropan is the original pioneer of modern quality Soave. His family have been producing wines for over 100 years from some of the best situated vineyards in the region. Fresh, zestful fruit and crisp acidity contrast with the texture of the squid and the intensity of the freshly squeezed lemon juice.

Chianti Rufina 1996, Fattoria Selvapiana, Tuscany – Northeast of Florence, along the Sieve valley, lies the Rufina zone. The valley is characterised by the cool sea breezes funnelled across the Appenines from the coast at Ravenna. Francesco Giuntini, whose family have owned Selvapiana since 1827, produces some of the most highly regarded wines and olive oil of the Rufina zone. Extra virgin olive oil from early picked Frantoio and Moraiolo olives is vibrantly green, peppery and intense. Wines from the area have a trademark high acidity which gives them great potential for aging and a dexterity in partnering the intense flavours of Tuscan cooking. The wines are nearly all made from Sangiovese vines growing in prime sites that catch the warmth of the day's sun while the cool winds moderate the temperature. This is the lightest and simplest of Selvapiana's wines but will still surprise with its complexity.

Recioto di Soave 'Le Colombare' 1995, Pieropan, Soave, Veneto – Intensely flavoured and delicately structured dessert wine. Late harvested Garganega and Trebbiano di Soave grapes are picked in October and placed in special drying rooms until January. During this time the grapes gently shrivel, intensifying their flavours as a result. Vinification of very small quantities involves maturation in various ly aged small oak casks. The intensity of the concentrated semi-dried grapes integrates with the smoke and spice of relatively young wood. An almost steely acidity provides the balance to the sweetness.

Metodo Franciacorta Cuvee Brut NV, Bellavista, Lombardia – The grapes used are 80% Chardonnay and 20% Pinot Bianco and Pinot Noir. Secondary fermentation takes place in the bottle known as the 'methode champenoise'. The gentle bitterness of the chocolate is complimented by the light biscuit quality of the spumante while the acidity combined with the fizz contrasts with the rich texture of the cake.

martin blunos

Martin Blunos used to have a restaurant in Bristol, in a graceless row of shops next to a laundrette. It was called Lettonie and had earned two Michelin stars and Martin thought no more of it, until a certain well-known restaurateur came to eat and commented on the 'poor' location.

In 1997, Martin moved Lettonie to a palatial Georgian house on the outskirts of Bath. There with his wife Siân, and their two sons Leon and Max, they could enjoy a real quality of life with the house and its gardens when the restaurant was closed two days a week. A move in November 2001 took Martin's cooking into the centre of Bath opening Blinis, so named after the blinis in his signature dish. He retained his two Michelin stars at the restaurant which is next to the river Avon, overlooking the famous weir below one of Bath's central landmarks; Pulteney Bridge. Robert Adam was commissioned to design Pulteney Bridge, modelled on Florence's Pont Vecchio in homage to Ancient Rome.

As you enter, and before you get to the restaurant, there is a blini bar where you can buy food related products by Martin as well as share and indulge in his passion for vodkas, blinis and Armagnacs.

In 2002, Siân took a well earned break from managing the restaurant, with the birth of their daughter Coco, whilst Martin teamed up with Sebastian and Phillipa Hughes of Chase Hotels and opened 'Martin Blunos at Fitzroys Brasserie' in their newly refurbished Duke's

Hotel in Bath, located just a short distance from Blinis along the magnificent Great Pulteney Street. He is proud that his two stars were awarded for what he did in the kitchen and not because of the front of house trappings. You could say he has done it the hard way, from pure talent alone. And he was honoured to be chosen to cook for the Queen at the Guildhall in Bath, when she visited in May 2002 on her jubilee tour.

When I first went to Bath to meet Martin Blunos, I was taken through the chefs' entrance into the Bonnet-sponsored kitchen and shown a little doorway leading to a smaller room, the effect decidedly 'Alice in Wonderland'. This impression grew when, at the other end, I caught a glimpse of Martin Blunos, larger than life with his walrus moustache. He noticed my plaster cast and got me to work straight away to see if I could cut a duck's egg with a broken wrist, going round the edge with a serrated knife. Blunos does not believe in people feeling sorry for themselves. There is a jovial atmosphere in the kitchen and, as a tonic for his six-strong staff, he keeps a boxing photograph on the kitchen wall with the inscription 'It's hard in the beginning'.

Blunos was born in England and has a strong West Country accent which belies his Latvian roots. Both his parents are from Latvia and, as well as the menu which counts an egg, caviar and vodka dish as a specialitiy, Lettonie is the French word for Latvia. Martin cannot speak Latvian, which is more akin to Lithuanian than Russian, but he can understand it. He has been to his parents' homeland once, when it was still occupied by the Russians. He noticed that there was not the usual 'embellishment' seen in the West; he remembers a bread van having nothing on its sides apart from, written

Richard Bramble 9

in plain bold red letters, B R E A D. He also remembers going out mushroom picking with his uncle's family. When they got back, they cooked a mushroom fricassee, but there was not enough for everyone – Martin was embarrassed when it was offered to him because you have to eat the food in Latvia when offered to you as a guest.

He now hears reports of new enterprise in free Latvia, in which people make food at home and go and sell it on street corners. The Latvian people have never had their own cuisine and it is only the second time in their history that they have had independence. In the capital, Riga, there is the statue of Mother Latvia (Milda). Milda holds three stars which represent the three 'cantons', or areas, the country had when it was split three ways on its independence; carved into the stone base of the statue are four corners which allude to the four decisive battles in the country's history.

'Milda is for freedom and fatherland ... she is weeping for her lost sons,' Martin told me late one night over a few Latvian beers. 'The Latvian flag is maroon with a white band. The first soldier fighting for independence was shot and all they could find to carry him home was a bed sheet. The women put his body on the sheet and carried him through the main streets of the city. When they took off his body his blood had soaked the sheet, apart from a white strip where he had been lying – hence the flag ... which is a load of old bollocks, but makes a great story.'

In his own words, Blunos takes Latvian 'peasant' dishes and transforms them for fine dining, such as his mother's chunky soup with a blob of sour cream, which is refined and made lighter. Blunos' classic signature dish is scrambled duck egg, still in its shell, topped with sevruga caviar. It is presented in a silver holder, coated in flaming vodka, accompanied by a plate of blinis and a glass of iced vodka – Lettonie offers you a selection of four vodkas at any one time. When I tried the dish I had lemon grass vodka and the combination hit the spot. Experimentation and a dab of amusement is never far from the big man's mind. On Valentine's Day a few years ago, they tried to create a dish between main course and dessert, in an attempt to get couples to look at the food and not into each other's eyes all the time. Martin's idea was for an ordinary empty egg shell which they secretly filled up with cream and mango purée – a dish they have since kept. This was presented to the diner as an unassuming boiled egg complete with shortbread 'soldiers'. It worked, as people started looking at their food for the first time that night; some even sent it back saying they had not ordered it. 'The presentation is the difference. Everything has been done before.'

He was always experimenting when he was young, his speciality being 'super hard rock cakes'. We talked about his early days as he showed me the garden, but not before I had tripped and fallen down a steep muddy bank causing his son to look at me as if I were one of the winos who frequent Bath's city centre. 'I used to enter Victoria Sandwich competitions at the local fete,' Martin told me, as I looked at my soiled trousers. The Blunoses' labrador, Amber, came and sat silently by my side, obviously at ease with my bucolic appearance. 'My parents thought I was going to grow up bent or something ... "not another bloody sponge-cake".'

He had no intention of becoming a chef, instead wanting to lay floors with his father. But his father had other ideas and told him to get a proper job. 'My dad suggested I do something with food because everyone's got to eat and I'll always have a job.'

Thinking ahead, Martin went straight to Switzerland to add kudos to his CV. When he arrived back in London, an agency took him on purely because he had been abroad – they did not even ask what, exactly, he had done in Switzerland. His first job was at The Strand Palace Hotel, opposite The Savoy. He lived in and liked being in the centre of London and having everything taken care of for him. 'There were nine-hundred bedrooms, loads of staff ... one floor full of girls, the one above, blokes – the place was rocking every night.'

Next he got a job in Greece, working on a yacht for a wealthy shipping magnate for six months. When he came back he started working in a little restaurant in Fulham, which is where he says 'the bug bit'. 'I started hanging round in the afternoons, not worried about how little money I was making, and started asking questions: why does this burn? Some afternoons Antony Worrall-Thompson would come in for a glass of wine and a chat with the owner.'

Gripped with passion, Blunos started working his way through a series of restaurants, on a constant quest to discover his own niche. In 1982 he found himself working in a restaurant on Queenstown Road by Battersea Park, when Nico and a few others were there and the area had a 'buzz' to it. This is where he met his wife, Siân. Martin told me that they hated each other at first and she tried to get him sacked. But, eventually, they got it all out of their systems and married. They both had their own flats and sold these to buy their first restaurant in 1988. As Martin has family in the West Country, and Siân's parents are from nearby Wales, they decided on the original restaurant in Bristol. It already had a star, but the main reason they bought it was because it had all the glassware and crockery in place, so they could open up after a 'lick of paint'. Martin's food kept up the Michelin standard, though there were no awards in the first year.

'We cooked from the heart rather than what the guide books want. Because we were living there the food was always good … the hardest thing for a restaurant is to be consistent.'

Bath is well known for its wild asparagus, allegedly brought over by the Romans as an aphrodisiac to encourage the local maidens. There is also a local trade in baby eel, caught from the River Severn during a relatively short period each year. The baby eels are expensive and, usually, exported to Japan, some batches fetching as much as £250,000.

If you think this sounds like money for old rope I might mention that the operation is rumoured to be 'controlled' Mafia-style.

Once I was taking photographs in Martins kitchen and had tentatively agreed to go up to the dining room at 8.30 to eat. Politeness got in the way and, at ten o'clock, I was still waiting for them to call me. They, in turn, were waiting for me. Anyway, I finally managed to sit down to eat and, later, joined Martin to try the Latvian beer he now imports from an old contact – this really is one of the best bottled beers I have tried. The next time I saw him I asked if I could take a bottle away to paint. Martin found it very funny that I was not direct enough to ask him for a bottle of beer to drink, so I suggested he gave me a crate. I'm still waiting.

166

borsch terrine

ingredients

1 kg (2 lb) large beetroot, peeled

500 g (1 lb) carrots, peeled

8 shallots, peeled

1 tsp caraway seeds

1 bay leaf

200 g (8 oz) shin of beef

8 leaves gelatine

Place all ingredients except the gelatine into a large pan, cover with cold water, bring to the boil and then skim. Place on the lid and simmer until the beetroot is cooked. Strain off the vegetables and meat, and put to one side. Bring the remaining juice back to the boil and reduce to 500 ml (1 pt) of cooking liquor. Soften the gelatine in cold water and melt into the hot liquor. Allow this to cool until it just begins to set. Meanwhile, slice the beetroot and carrots into inch slices.

Pour a little of the unset jelly into a 500 ml (1 pt) loaf tin, then add a layer of beetroot slices. Season with a little salt and pepper, then pour on a little more unset jelly. Add a layer of carrot slices, seasoning, jelly, and then the shallots in a row down the centre. Season once more. Add a further layer of jelly, carrots and seasoning before finally finishing with a layer of beetroot. Cover with film and press with a heavy chopping board. Place in the fridge until set.

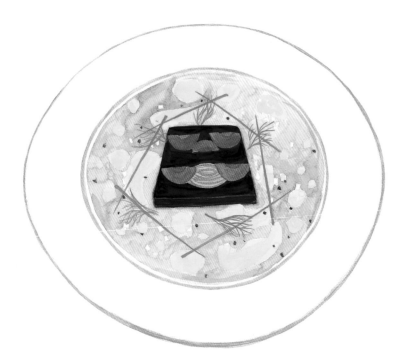

 Eden Valley Australian Riesling 1989

167

"Acipenser stellatus - Sevruga sturgeon"

Sevruga sturgeon - 'Acipenser stellatus - Living for 40 years, spawns after 8 years, weight 25 kg, length 1½ m

"Acipenser stellatus - Sevruga sturgeon"

Oscietra sturgeon - 'Acipenser guldenstadii' - Living for 60 years, spawns after 12 years, weight 200 kg, length 2m.

"Huso huso - Beluga Sturgeon"

Beluga sturgeon - 'Huso huso' - Living for 100 years, spawns after 18 years, weight 1000 kg, length 4½ m.

Caviar is the roe of the Sturgeon fish native to the northern hemisphere, a survivor from the Triassic period originating some 250 million years ago. The second oldest species of fish in the world, the shark being the first. During the Roman occupation of Britain there was a sturgeon farm in Wales which supplied the emperor, and wild sturgeon could still be caught. Today sturgeon stocks are increasly threatened by overfishing and the destruction of the habitat. The main and only real source is the Caspian Sea and its river systems. The demise of the U.S.S.R has led to the regional mafiosi on the Russian side controlling things in an unmanaged way. 'Shilat' - the Iranian state body which fishes is carefully controlled and managed. The Iranian caviar is better as the fish are netted in boats earlier in the season when the sea is cooler and the eggs firmer. They also never mix eggs from one fish with another like the Russians. Russians net across the deltas as the sturgeon are trying to swim up the rivers to spawn. The roe is almost over ripe and the Volga river is now heavily polluted. There are three species of sturgeon that produce caviar; Beluga the largest and most expensive. Only 2% of the catch is beluga. It is the only carn vorous of the three, the eggs are steely grey in colour, large in size and taste delicate with hint of walnut. Called 'Imperial' or 'Royal' the egg come in a blue tin. Osietr are slightly smaller and considered first in flavour by many. Variegated colours of browns, and golder the older the fish. Taste varies as it is a bottom feeder, a nutty flavour. The Sevruga is the smallest are dark grey and have a distinctive taste of the sea.
  The curing process is simple, the eggs are removed, cleaned of the surrounding membrane and salt and borax, a preservative, added. Caviar will keep in unopened tins at 3°C for 2 months. It can be frozen, thaw out in a fridge slowly. Pasteurised caviar has hardened eggs and an inferior taste. Serve caviar with a bone spoon as silver reacts with it. The future for the sturgeon is uncertain. Beluga is facing extinction. The Iranians are releasing many hatchling sturgeon back into the Caspian Sea and they are being farmed in Bordeaux. Uncontrolled Russian fishing is damaging stocks and needs to be regulated.

scrambled duck egg

ingredients

4 fresh duck eggs

2 large hen eggs

3 tbsp chilled water

5 turns white pepper

2 tbsp clarified unsalted butter

4 heaped teaspoons caviar
(Beluga or Sevruga)

4 cleaned duck egg shells

SERVES 4

Whisk together all the eggs with the chilled water and the white pepper. Heat the clarified butter in a thick-bottomed pan, pour in the egg mixture and stir constantly with a spatula until creamy, thick, and a soft scramble is achieved. Do not overcook the eggs at this stage, as the flambe will finish them off. Spoon the scrambled egg into the clean, empty shells and level off with the back of a knife. Spoon on the caviar and dome up neatly.

To serve, pour a little warmed vodka into a serving plate, stand the egg in the middle and flambé. Serve with warm blinis and a glass of iced vodka.

steamed stuffed fillet of gilt-head seabream

ingredients

4 x 300 g (10 oz) fillets
of bream

250 g (9 oz) salmon flesh

4 large fresh scallops, diced

1 large egg

1 pinch cayenne pepper

1 pinch salt

2 tsp lemon juice

100 ml (3 fl oz) double cream

SERVES 4

In a food processor, mix the salmon, egg, lemon juice and seasoning until smooth. Pass through a fine sieve. Return to the processor bowl, add the cream and blend until well combined. Fold in the diced scallops, and put the whole mixture in the fridge.

To prepare the fillets, lay them on a board, skin side down. Cut along the central seam of the fillet and slide first to the left of the fillet (without cutting through to the end) and then repeat on the right. Open up the fillet, spoon a little of the chilled mousse on the middle of the open fillet, then cover with the flaps and wrap in cling film to seal. Place on a steamer for 8 minutes, remove cling film, season the flesh side with lemon juice, salt and pepper, and serve.

 Aotea Cabernet Sauvignon Pinotage 1996

boiled egg and soldiers

ingredients

clean egg shells

For the Mango Purée

1 ripe mango

caster sugar to taste

lemon juice to taste

For the Vanilla Cream

250 ml (8 fl oz) full fat milk

50 g (2 oz) caster sugar

1 vanilla pod

3 medium egg yolks

25 g (1 oz) plain flour

250 ml (8 fl oz) double cream

For the Soldiers

100 g (3½ oz) plain flour

100 g (3½ oz) rice flour

100 g (3½ oz) caster sugar

100 g (3½ oz) unsalted butter

1 medium egg, beaten

pinch of salt

To make the soldiers, sieve the flours and the salt into a bowl. Rub the butter until you have a breadcrumb texture. Mix in the sugar. Bind with the egg until you have a stiff paste. Press the mixture into a tin to a depth of 1 in. Bake in the oven at 175°C/350°F/Gas Mark 4 for about 20 minutes until golden brown. Turn out while hot and cut quickly into fingers. Cool on a rack and, when cold, store in an airtight container.

For the mango purée, peel and de-stone the mango and liquidise until smooth. Add the lemon juice and sugar to taste. Pass through a fine strainer and store in fridge until needed.

Now make the vanilla cream. Beat the yolks, sugar, salt and flour until pale. Bring the milk, flavoured with the vanilla pod, to just before boiling point. Pour onto the yolk mix, then transfer to a clean pan, stir until boiling point and then pass through a fine strainer. Cover and cool. Whip the cream until it makes soft peaks and fold it into the cold vanilla mixture.

To serve, place a little of the mango purée in the bottom of the clean egg shell. Cover with vanilla cream and place some more mango on top to resemble the egg yolk. Place the biscuits on the side of the plate with granulated sugar and grated chocolate to resemble the salt and pepper.

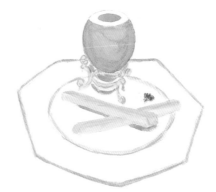

 Essencia Orange Muscat 1995, Quady, California

apple parfait

For the Parfait

1 kg (3 lb) Bramley apples

lemon juice

4 medium egg yolks

85 g (3 oz) caster sugar

250 ml (8 fl oz) double cream

2 tbsp calvados

For the Crumb Mix

100 g (3½ oz) plain flour

50 g (2 oz) unsalted butter

25 g (1 oz) caster sugar

1 level tsp mixed spice

pinch of salt

Peel the apples and roughly chop them. Add the lemon juice and cook gently until soft. Purée in a liquidiser and then pass through a fine sieve. Allow to cool, and then chill in the fridge.

Use a mixer to beat the egg yolks until pale. Place the sugar and a little water in a pan, and then boil until syrupy. Pour onto the egg yolks with the mixer still turning (note that the syrup is very hot). Continue to beat until cool and thick. Whip the double cream with the calvados until it is the same thickness as the syrup and egg mix. Fold the two together until well combined.

Spoon a layer of the cream mix into a 500 g (1 lb) loaf tin, levelling with the back of a spatula, then add a thin layer of the apple purée. Repeat the process until the loaf tin is full. Gently tap the tin to release any air pockets. Cover with film and freeze for a minimum of 24 hours.

Now, make a sorbet with the remaining apple purée by adding to it one third of its volume of sugar syrup (equal quantities of sugar and water brought to the boil and cooled). Adjust the tartness with a little lemon juice and then freeze, stirring from time to time until set.

To make the crumb, sieve the flour, spice and salt into a bowl. Add the sugar and rub in the butter until it has a crumbly texture. Spread on a baking tray. Cook in an oven at 175°C/350°F/Gas Mark 4 until crisp and golden. Cool on a tray and then store in an airtight container.

To serve, arrange a ring of crumbs on the outside of a plate. Turn out the parfait and cut a slice: place this in the centre of the plate. Place 3 balls of sorbet around on the crumbs. Garnish and serve.

 Veuve Clicquot White Label Demi Sec Champagne

Veuve Clicquot White Label champagne — From the large, prestigious house whose success was founded by 'The Widow' Clicquot, who took over the business in 1805 at the age of 27 when her husband died. She invented the now universal 'remuage' system for clarifying wine and produced the first rosé. Velvety soft and luscious this demi-sec champagne would complement and not compete with the apple flavours.

Aotea Cabernet Sauvignon-Pinotage 96, Hawkes Bay New Zealand — Comes from one of the top quality regions, situated on the east coast south of Gisborne, and in the rain shadow of the Island's volcanic mountain centre. Its sunshine and its mixture of soils — silt, shingle and clay provide enormous potential. A wonderful wine with light rose colour, clean cassis and berry flavours to match with the Bream.

Essencia Orange Muscat 95 Quady, California, — Based at Madera the Quady winery was founded in 1977 by the principal and wine maker Andrew Quady. From the classic Portuguese varieties of grape he has planted, comes a range of dessert wines and ports. The celebrated Essencia is from the Orange Muscat grape. With its orange blossom and honey raisins taste it is also good with chocolate and even chèvre cheese.

Eden Valley Australian Riesling 1989 Temple Bruer, South Australia — The wine maker Bruer is an expert, and has a technical background having lectured on wine at Roseworthy college. He does not believe in using too many insecticides, instead opens the flood gates onto the Angus River and "Drowns the bastards". This is a luscious and aromatic handmade wine with flavours of lime and passion fruit. Will keep for 10 years, but drinkable after.

pierre koffmann

Every gastronome knows that Pierre Koffmann's signature dish is his pig's trotters – he designed the dish and now others copy it. When I first met him I showed my ignorance by looking him straight in the eye and asking him what his speciality was as I would feature it in a painting. After that he gave me the impression that he was tolerating me, which is hardly surprising as chefs of this calibre and standing expect you at least to have done some basic research. With hindsight, preparation should have been a priority, knowing how difficult it is to get to know him.

I first met his manager, Patrice, when I asked if I could work on a painting of the outside of La Tante Claire – it really was a beautiful setting nestled in the heart of the botanical garden enclave of Chelsea. One day while I was painting, a beautiful lady dashed out of the restaurant and down the street, struggling to keep her balance on her high-heeled shoes. She looked back once, to the paparazzi photographer who had appeared from behind a hedge. When I saw the all-too-familiar hounded expression on her face I knew immediately it was Princess Diana. Within seconds a black Range Rover pulled up to whisk her away to the 'safety' of the Royal security cocoon. I was still thinking about this when my cousin, David, walked past, apparently unaware who I was until I shouted after him. In fairness, I was togged up against the crisp November day, wearing four jumpers and a large woolly hat. This particular hat alters the shape of a person's head so much that it would be well worth the Army considering it as part of any future camouflage strategy. I am certainly not famous, but even I enjoy the

odd moment of anonymity, when I can disapear into the background and observe and paint without even friends knowing who I am. Matisse liked the idea that some Japanese artists changed their names and identities throughout their careers, to avoid the distractions that come with recognition, and to protect their freedom.

As far as Pierre was concerned I only saw him once while I was painting, and he did not come over to say hello. When I finally got a chance to sit down and show him the picture it was a very abrupt meeting with his not giving much away. Sometimes, however, he can be quite chatty, not at all reserved – it all depends on which day you catch him. It was not the best day not to know about his signature dish – it takes a long time to win someone's confidence after that. A year later I went back to paint Pierre in his kitchen and he was quite jovial; on the next occasion he could not remember who I was, though he did become more receptive when he saw the finished painting and thought I had made him look ten years younger.

As chef patron, Pierre Koffmann spends most of his kitchen time teaching others how to cook dishes; sometimes he plays a psychological game with the minds of his top chefs. For example, I once saw an experienced chef make the mistake of not having the sauce ready for a dish. He was sent down to scrub out the cellars – as far as I know, he has not forgotten the sauce again.

Pierre Koffmann was born in the city of Tarbes in south west France in 1948, the second of four children. He attributes much of his cooking to the taste of the food he ate as a boy and to the influence of his maternal grandparents, Camille and Marcel Cadeillan, and their teaching him all about the seasons, animals and crops, and ploughing and harvesting on their small farm in a village in Gascony. Seasons were important with the whole village typically eating paschal lamb at Easter, harvest lunches of *poule au pot* in the summer, hares, pheasants and delicious little ortolans in the autumn, and ducks, geese and

pigs in the winter. In his book, *Memories of Gascony*, Koffmann says that his grandmother's cooking was 'typical peasant cooking of the Gers', in which the people lived off the land and any food bought from a shop was considered an unnecessary extravagance.

Koffmann later attended the Ecole Hotelière de Tarbes and spent several years working in different restaurants in France and Switzerland: Juan les Pins on the Côte d'Azur and others in Strasbourg and Lausanne. In 1971 he saw in *L'Hotellerie* that Le Gavroche needed a commis chef, so he came to England. He soon progressed to chef de partie and was transferred to Brasserie Benoits before it became Le Gamin. He left to work for the Cazalets for a while and then returned to the Roux brothers for the opening of The Waterside Inn in 1972. He stayed here as chef de cuisine, seeing its first Michelin star in 1973 and its second in 1974. Koffmann had always wanted his own restaurant and in 1977, after a false start in France, he and his wife opened La Tante Claire, a small, warm, and very enticing restaurant named after an aunt with a penchant for cooking and good food. It had two Michelin

stars within a few years, eventually obtaining the hallowed three stars. Its most recent transition is the move to the Berkeley Hotel, which has doubled the covers and provided Pierre with his next challenge.

He is aware of the dialogue between country cooking and the great tradition of court cooking, or grande cuisine, and thinks the contrast has created what we now have in modern cuisine with all the refinement but a healthy respect for natural flavours. Perhaps most of all Pierre Koffmann remembers his grandfather's 'partnership' with the land and his wisdom in having the patience not to try to rush or meddle with the unalterable ways of nature.

truffle tart

ingredients

25 g (1 oz) puff pastry

40 g (1½ oz) celeriac purée

20 g (¾ oz) black truffle, thinly sliced

1 tbsp truffle oil

1 tsp balsamic vinegar

pinch of sea salt

SERVES 1

Pre-heat the oven to 200°C/400°F/Gas Mark 6. Roll out the pastry very thinly, cut a 15 cm circle, and place between two heavy baking trays on silicon mats. Bake for 10 minutes and then remove and cool.

Now heat the celeriac purée and spoon it onto the baked pastry disc so that it covers the entire circle right to the edge. Arrange the truffle slices on the top of the pastry, overlapping them slowly. Place in the oven for 1 minute to warm. Sprinkle the top with sea salt and serve with a green salad.

 Pinot Gris, Les Princes Abbes 1995 Domaine Schlumberger

stuffed pigs' trotters with morels

SERVES 4

ingredients

4 pigs' back trotters, boned

100 g (3½ oz) carrots, diced

100 g (3½ oz) onions, diced

150 ml (5 fl oz) dry white wine

1 tbsp port

150 ml (5 fl oz) veal stock

225 g (8 oz) veal sweetbreads, blanched and chopped

75 g (3 oz) butter, plus a knob for the sauce

20 dried morels, soaked until soft

1 small onion, finely chopped

1 chicken breast, skinned and diced

1 egg white

200 ml (7 fl oz) double cream

salt and pepper

Preheat the oven to 160°C/325°F/Gas Mark 3.

Place the trotters in a casserole with the diced carrots and onions, the wine, port and veal stock. Cover and cook in the oven for 3 hours.

Meanwhile, fry the sweetbreads in the butter for 5 minutes, add the morels and chopped onion and cook for another 5 minutes. Leave to cool.

Purée the chicken breast with the egg white and cream and season with salt and pepper. Mix with the sweetbread mixture to make the stuffing. Take the trotters out of the casserole and strain the cooking stock, keeping the stock but discarding the vegetables. Open the trotters out flat and lay each one on a piece of foil. Leave to cool.

Fill the cooled trotters with the chicken stuffing and roll tightly in the foil. Chill in the fridge for at least 2 hours.

Now, preheat the oven to 220°C/425°F/Gas Mark 7. Put the foil-wrapped trotters in a casserole, cover and heat in the oven for 15 minutes.

Put the trotters on a serving dish and remove the foil. Pour the reserved stock into the casserole and reduce by half. Whisk in a knob of butter, pour the sauce over the trotters and serve very hot.

Madiran 1989 Château Peyrus

180

'Pecten maximus'

Scallops are molluscs that filter feed on the bottom of the sea bed and move around by clapping shut their shells and being propelled backwards. They do this either to more feeding grounds or to try and escape predators such as the star fish. They partly bury themselves as camouflage and their shells also somewhat take on the colouration of their surroundings.

They are gathered in the wild by dredging the bottom or by divers hand picking them. The former must be stopped as it destroys the bottom of the sea bed indiscriminately killing all in its path. The scallops caught this way are damaged and gritty and should be avoided. The best and biggest come from the west coasts of Scotland and Ireland, where it is still possible to snorkel for them at spring low tides.

A fresh scallop will snap shut when handled, and the meat will smell sweet. To open place the rounded shell in the palm of your hand, place the tip of a long narrow knife in the gap on the sides of the shells and cut the muscle which is attached to the upper flat shell. The shell will open and remove the white muscle and orange coral discarding everything else. The coral is the digestive and reproductive part, it is stronger tasting. It is sometimes left out of recipes for this reason, but it has a vibrant orange colour that begs to be included. The white muscle from larger scallops can be cut in half before cooking. They cook very quickly and contain a lot of sugar and caramelise well. I have found that freshly caught, they are wonderful placed back in their cleaned shells seasoned with a little cream and grilled. Or rolled in seasoned flour and pan fried in virgin olive oil.

The scallop shell is associated with the birth of Venus, who rode in one and St James, whose pilgrims wore a shell badge on their broad-brimmed hats whilst on pilgrimage to Santiago de Compostela in Spain. The reason being, the story goes, the body of St James was being returned to Galicia borne in a boat with no oars or sail. As it was passing a village called Padron nearby to Santiago de Compostela, a bridegroom was riding his horse on the beach when he was suddenly dragged into the sea by the panicky horse. To the amazement of his friends they surfaced beside the boat. Having been converted they returned to the shore, both the horse and rider covered in scallop shells.

scallops with squid ink, red pepper and garlic sauces

ingredients

12 very fresh scallops

For the Squid Ink Sauce

50 ml (2 fl oz) dry vermouth

100 ml (4 fl oz) double cream

50 g (2 oz) shallots, chopped

1 small garlic clove, chopped

1 tsp squid ink

salt and pepper

For the Red Pepper Sauce

½ red pepper, thinly sliced

50 ml (2 fl oz) whipping cream

For the Garlic Sauce

2 garlic cloves, chopped

50 ml (2 fl oz) whipping cream

SERVES 4

First make the squid ink sauce by combining all the ingredients except the seasoning in a small pan. Reduce by half, season, process in a blender until smooth and then pass through a fine sieve. Keep warm.

Now make the red pepper sauce by putting the pepper and the cream in a small pan and reducing to 4 tablespoons of sauce. Season and process in a blender until smooth, then pass through a fine sieve. Keep warm.

Now make the garlic sauce. Put the garlic and cream in a small pan and reduce to about 4 tablespoons of sauce. Season, process in a blender, then pass through a fine sieve. Keep warm.

Halve the scallops widthways and season on both sides. Cook briefly on both sides in a non-stick pan until nicely brown. Keep warm. In the middle of 4 warm plates, pour first the ink sauce, then a tablespoon each of the pepper and garlic sauce. Arrange 6 slices of scallops on these sauces.

 Pernand Vergelesse 1993 Marius Delarche

fillets of venison with raspberry vinegar and bitter chocolate sauce

SERVES 4

ingredients

4 x 150 g (5 oz) venison fillets

2 tbsp vegetable oil

1 tsp finely chopped shallots

25 ml (1 fl oz) raspberry vinegar

500 ml (18 fl oz) red wine

150 ml (5 fl oz) venison stock

50 g (2 oz) bitter chocolate

30 g (1 oz) butter

salt and pepper

Heat the oil in a frying pan. When very hot, cook the venison to taste, making sure they are brown all over. Season, transfer to a plate and keep warm. Tip all the fat out of the pan and then fry the shallots until soft. Deglaze with the vinegar and let it reduce completely. Add the red wine and reduce to about a quarter. Add the stock and bitter chocolate. When it has melted, whisk in the butter. Slice the venison fillets and serve with the sauce poured over.

 Collioure Domaine de la Rectorie Parce Frère 1993

salmon cooked in goose fat

ingredients

4 x 150 g (5 oz) salmon fillets, skinned

250 g (9 oz) goose fat

100 g (3½ oz) onions, sliced

2 red peppers, skinned and de-seeded, cut into 2 cm (¾ in) squares

1 garlic clove, crushed

6 large tomatoes, peeled, deseeded and diced

salt and pepper

4 thin slices parma ham

course salt, for serving

SERVES 4

Heat 25 g (1 oz) goose fat in a frying pan, add the onions and cook gently for 10 minutes without letting them colour. Add the peppers and cook for 3 minutes, then add the garlic and tomatoes and cook for 5 minutes. Season to taste and keep hot.

In a deep saucepan, gently heat the remaining fat to 50°C/122°F (no hotter, or the salmon will dry out). Put in the salmon fillets (the fat should cover the fish completely) and cook for 7-10 minutes, depending on the thickness of the fillets. The salmon is ready when you can pierce it easily with a chef's fork. Place the salmon on a plate, cover with greaseproof paper and leave to rest in a warm place for 10 minutes.

Arrange the vegetable garnish in a serving dish and lay the salmon fillets on top. In a frying pan, fry the ham for 10 seconds on each side in a little hot goose fat, lay the slices over the fish and serve with a dish of coarse salt.

 Saumur Blanc 1994 Pierre de Bruyn

pistachio soufflé

ingredients

100 ml (3 fl oz) milk

50 g (2 oz) pistachio paste

1 egg

1 extra egg yolk

50 g (2 oz) caster sugar

40 g (1½ oz) plain flour

20 g (¾ oz) butter, softened

50 g (2 oz) grated chocolate

6 egg whites

SERVES 6

Preheat the oven to 230°C/450°F/Gas Mark 8. Boil the milk with the pistachio paste. Beat together the egg, the egg yolk and half the sugar for two minutes, then add the flour and mix for 1 minute. Pour on the milk mixture, transfer to a saucepan and cook for four minutes, whisking continuously. Pour the mixture into a bowl, cover with foil and keep in a warm place.

Grease the inside of 6 individual soufflé dishes with the softened butter, and coat with grated chocolate. Now, beat the egg whites very stiffly, add the remaining sugar and beat until firm. Whisk the pistachio mixture for a few seconds, then add a quarter of the egg whites and whisk it in vigorously. Add half the remaining egg whites, stirring quickly with a spatula to make sure there are no lumps. Quickly stir in the rest of the egg whites in the same way.

Pour the soufflé mixture into the prepared dishes and bake in the preheated oven for 10 minutes. Serve with pistachio ice cream.

 Jurançon Moelleux 1995 Casterras

aaron patterson

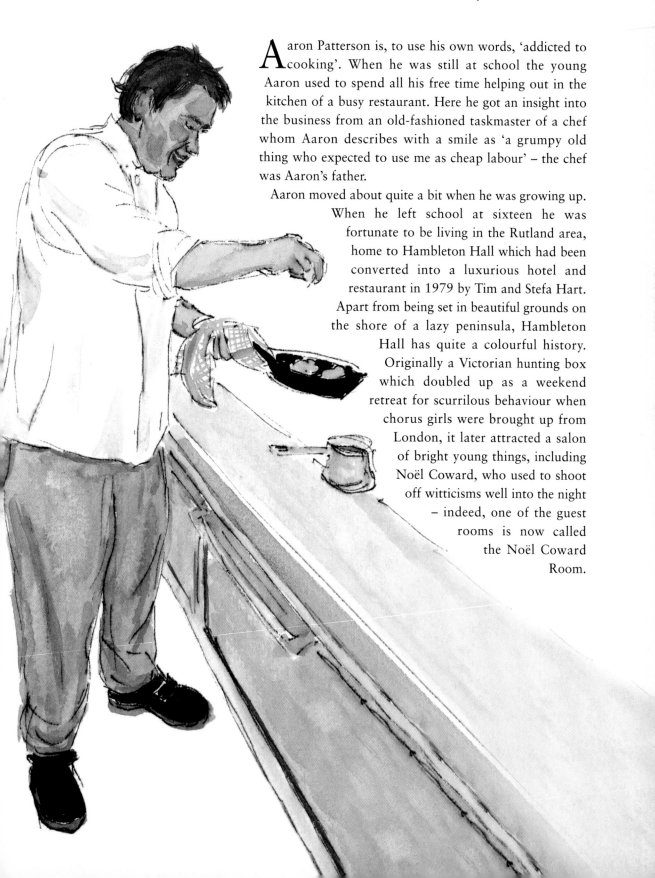

Aaron Patterson is, to use his own words, 'addicted to cooking'. When he was still at school the young Aaron used to spend all his free time helping out in the kitchen of a busy restaurant. Here he got an insight into the business from an old-fashioned taskmaster of a chef whom Aaron describes with a smile as 'a grumpy old thing who expected to use me as cheap labour' – the chef was Aaron's father.

Aaron moved about quite a bit when he was growing up. When he left school at sixteen he was fortunate to be living in the Rutland area, home to Hambleton Hall which had been converted into a luxurious hotel and restaurant in 1979 by Tim and Stefa Hart. Apart from being set in beautiful grounds on the shore of a lazy peninsula, Hambleton Hall has quite a colourful history. Originally a Victorian hunting box which doubled up as a weekend retreat for scurrilous behaviour when chorus girls were brought up from London, it later attracted a salon of bright young things, including Noël Coward, who used to shoot off witticisms well into the night – indeed, one of the guest rooms is now called the Noël Coward Room.

Still chiselled in the stone arch above the front door at Hambleton Hall are the words of Francois Rabelais (c.1494-1553) used as a motto by the 18th century Hell Fire Club, which used to gather to celebrate women and wine: Fay Ce Que Voudras, meaning 'do as you please' in old French. Perhaps Aaron thought he might be in for a spot of misrule when he first arrived for an interview; he actually found himself immediately head down and hard at work in the kitchen.

At the time, Tim Hart

had managed to get hold of A A Gill's brother, Nick Gill, as his head chef. Aaron, finding Nick an inspiration, but lacking in discipline, set about motivating himself, relentlessly developing his skills in all the kitchen departments and giving Tim cause to remember him as 'someone who stood out immediately, the best person we'd had'.

After five years, Aaron decided he should gain experience somewhere else and went to work under Raymond Blanc. Aaron eventually returned to Hambleton Hall before his twenty-fourth birthday to replace Gill as head chef.

Tim Hart, previously in the city as an investment banker, is used to taking calculated risks, but admits it was quite a gamble placing someone so young in such a position of authority over an established reputation. Aaron Patterson paid off and within three months all the top food critics were paying homage to this new star. Another quality Tim noticed in Aaron was his 'very unusual combination of leadership skills'. At the time the kitchen was very small and tempers frayed easily; the head chef needs a certain maturity to stay on top of the situation. Since then Hambleton Hall's kitchen has undergone a massive refurbishment and now has a brigade of eleven. Once you get to this size you need to be, as well as an exceptional chef, a good organiser and inspirational chief. In a top kitchen everything is important and what at first can seem a mole hill can all too quickly turn into a mountain. The responsibility rests with the head chef. For example, he cannot afford to get his ordering even slightly out: the freshness of a fine menu is very unforgiving and will not allow for any compensation of ingredients.

I asked Aaron about the role of leader. 'I was thrown in at the deep end quite early on ... I had to learn management skills, how to use a computer, do the accounts. As far as people skills are concerned, I think you have to use your intelligence. Look at how you've been treated and work out how you would have liked to have been treated. When I started I wanted to give a hundred per cent. Nick Gill was a talent ... he helped me creatively. At another place I worked under a head chef who ran the kitchen like a sergeant major ... great discipline, but no creativity in the cooking. So now, with my junior chefs, I try to be inspirational and to keep discipline ... you have to take the best from everyone you've worked with.'

It is true that young chefs are easily influenced, particularly if the head chef is what is referred to as 'hard'. Such chefs can rot the barrel, as it were, creating a next generation of hard chefs, who in turn ... it can become a vicious circle.

I have watched Aaron's cooking quite closely while painting his dishes and it is obvious his main inspiration is the ingredients. His starting point is always to find the right raw materials, find the best money can buy, local wherever possible. One local supplier is Jan McCourt at Northfield Farm who, with his wife Tessa, has the largest herd of rare breed Dexter cows in England. The Dexter is a small, short-legged cow, believed to have come from Ireland, which produces truly succulent beef and is one of the few breeds never to have had BSE. Rare breeds are the old

le temps passe l'amitié reste
c'est l'heure de bien faire

farm animals that had been developed by farming predecessors for their eating qualities. Old-fashioned breeds are not cheap to produce and take time to mature – Dexter beef is hung for at least three weeks. At Northfield Farm all animals are naturally reared and the breed, age and diet of every piece of meat supplied is known.

Aaron told me about the first time he met Jan. 'When Jan arrived it was in the middle of a busy service. I thought, go away, another supplier. But when I saw the beef, I thought it looked really good. I sliced off a piece … like nothing I'd ever tasted … it's incredible … when you find something like this, which nobody else has, that's really special, isn't it?'

And Aaron is never afraid to try something new. Jan once brought in a monstrous piece of hogget – neither lamb nor mutton – from one of his grey-faced Dartmoor sheep. 'I looked at it … it was quite fatty. I told Jan I'll see what I can do.'

After immersing it in a vat of hand-hot oil for two days, the meat had a taste that was out of this world.

Aaron is now Jan's main customer. The link between Aaron and his suppliers is very close, all of them liking him not just for his custom, but for his personality. Aaron reminds me of Peter Pan, instantly likeable and someone who will look forever young. And Aaron likes to get involved. Another local supplier is something of a colourful character, who finds time to teach fishing in the summer despite having eight children. 'He brings me the most fantastic game in winter … prepares it as well. He also brings in wild mushrooms, pike, watercress … he's worth his weight in gold … great guy.'

In Scotland, Aaron has someone who dives for scallops especially for him. Closer to home, John Houghton, whose family have been farming in the area for 400 years, grows asparagus in clay soil, making it particularly rich in goodness. Everything is extra fresh at Hambleton Hall, and the customers are more aware of where things have come from. The produce from the soil of Hambleton garden actually tastes authentic. There is a lovely story of the time when an order came in for a dessert requiring apricots and the kitchen discovered none had been picked. One of the commis chefs was sent outside to select a few straight from the tree. Within 15 minutes the diner had his pudding in front of him – it does not get much fresher than that.

'That's what it's about.' Aaron looked at me with his characteristic full-face smile. 'I love it here … why would I want to move? White peaches are grown against a south-facing wall. In the summer I'll go and play tennis, then sit

down and stuff myself with peaches ... amazing.' The smile had not faded.

Aaron believes in good working conditions and good training in the kitchen. There is a family atmosphere at Hambleton Hall and staff regularly do things together, including enjoying a pint at the nearby village pub, The Finches. 'Chefs don't come here for the money. They're impressed by the ingredients and the kitchen ... they appreciate what we're trying to achieve here. I've never had a problem with staff.'

When Aaron has a chef coming in for an

pastry chef

RB 98

interview he generously makes them feel at home, gives them lunch and discusses the food in detail – he wants enthusiastic chefs. Hambleton Hall attracts not only the best, but some of the most interesting people at all levels.

Aaron now has a business interest in Hambleton Hall. Everybody knows that he could earn twice as much in London, but Tim Hart is about as good as they get as far as business partners go and the quality of life Aaron has with his wife and family more than compensates. The arrangement also incudes Tim's wonderful new designer brasserie in Nottingham called Hart's, built on the site of the old General Hospital. It is perched on a hill above the city in a similar way the Acropolis is raised above Athens – indeed, nearby there is a small neo-classical building reminiscent of the Temple of Nike. Inside the restaurant, the walls are hung with paintings by Tim's father-in-law, Vladimir Dascaloff, who in the 1960s tried to relate colour to music, to express tunes visually.

No matter how successful business plans are, Aaron's main mission will always be to be the best chef he can be. 'I'll always work in the kitchen … I look forward to getting up in the morning and getting to the kitchen. I couldn't

ponce about pretending to be an executive chef … I'm addicted to food … that's it.'

Among the community of top chefs a second Michelin star is a benchmark they all care about – Aaron is no exception. Tim Hart is more philosophical: 'Aaron is already cooking at a very high level which would put us in the top ten in many people's books – we are in all the top guides. I believe in having your own standards – one's cooking should not reflect the expectations of others.'

Aaron Patterson has come a long way in a short space of time, unusually without ever having worked in a kitchen in France. He has featured in a Channel Four series on his cooking, and people say he is a natural in front of the camera; he is a chef who learns quickly and applies his skills persistently to achieve his goals. Perhaps certain things have already come full circle for Aaron.

I have met Aaron's elder brother, who is a graphic designer, by chance, when he popped into the kitchen for an impromptu meal. He told me that both he and Aaron used to work in their father's restaurant. Being the elder of the two, he was given the front of house duties – he would have preferred to cook.

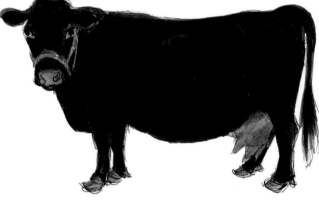

mediterranean vegetable terrine

MAKES 18-20 SLICES

Peel, de-seed and slice the peppers, then roast them for 8-10 minutes until soft. Slice and roast the aubergines in a slow oven until soft. Cook the artichokes for 15-20 minutes in boiling water with a little lemon juice, garlic and thyme. Peel away the leaves and remove the hearts. Quarter the courgettes and cook them in boiling water for about 5 minutes.

Layer the vegetables in a 30 cm x 8 cm x 6 cm terrine, using the tomato jelly in-between each layer. Leave to set overnight.

 1995 Petite Arvine, Valais Canton, Cave Imesch Sierre

ingredients
For the Terrine
450 g (1 lb) red peppers
450 g (1 lb) yellow peppers
2.4 kg (5 lb 5 oz) aubergines
1.5 kg (3 lb 5 oz) plum tomatoes, liquidised and set with leaf gelatine (8 leaves to 1 litre of tomato)
5 large artichokes
800 g (1 lb 12 oz) courgettes, quartered

loin of hare wrapped in puff pastry with red wine sauce

ingredients

1 loin of hare

puff pastry

red wine sauce

For the Red Cabbage

1 large red cabbage, shredded

750 ml (1 pt 5 fl oz) cider

375 ml (12 fl oz) port

375 ml (12 fl oz) red wine

10 g (½ oz) star anise

5 g (¼ oz) cinnamon sticks

5 g (¼ oz) whole cardamom pods

200 ml (7 fl oz) balsamic vinegar

SERVES 1

To prepare the red cabbage, tie the star anise, cinammon and cardamom in muslin. Mix all the alcohol in a saucepan, add the muslin and bring slowly to the boil. Now pour the alcohol over the shredded cabbage and leave for 24 hours. When this has been done, bring the cabbage and alcohol to a very gentle simmer and cook until all the liquid has evaporated and the cabbage is soft. Note that once it is cooked, the cabbage can be bottled and kept in the fridge for weeks.

The loin of hare should be stripped from the bone. Wrap it in a square of puff pastry and cook in a hot oven for 8 minutes, 4 minutes on each side. Garnish with red cabbage and a selection of root vegetables and the red wine sauce.

 Pic Saint Loup Domaine de L'Hortus, Jean Orliac 1996

roast sirloin of dexter beef

200 g (7 oz) sirloin Dexter beef

red wine sauce

For the Fondant Potatoes

750 g (1 lb 10 oz) potatoes

60 g (2 oz) butter

clove of garlic

sprig of rosemary

SERVES 1

To make the fondant potatoes, peel and slice the potatoes so that they are about 3 cm thick. Put them in a small thick-bottomed pan with the butter, garlic and rosemary, cover with water and season. Cook on a high heat until the water has evaporated and the potato is coloured. Turn over and colour the other side and then finish in a slow oven for 5-10 minutes.

Roast the Dexter beef for about 10-12 minutes at 190°C/375°F/Gas Mark 5 until medium rare.

Serve with the potatoes and a red wine sauce.

 1994 Frog's Leap Winery, Zinfandel, John Williams Napa

chocolate pavé

ingredients

For the Pavé Sponge

100 g (3½ oz) cocoa powder

150 g (5 oz) icing sugar

6 eggs

For the White Chocolate Mousse

200 g (7 oz) crème patissière

400 g (14 oz) white chocolate

600 ml (1 pt) double cream, semi-whipped

For the Dark Chocolate Mousse

300 g (10½ oz) dark chocolate

125 ml (4 fl oz) hot coffee

6 egg yolks

300 ml (½ pt) whipping cream, semi-whipped

For the Raspberry Sorbet

750 g (1 lb 10 oz) sugar

660 ml (22 fl oz) water

3 oz liquid glucose

3 punnets raspberries

SERVES 8

First, make the sorbet. Dissolve the sugar, water and glucose, bring to the boil and boil for 3 minutes. Now purée the raspberries and pass them through a fine sieve. Put the raspberries (keeping a few aside for presentation) in a bowl and gradually mix in the sorbet syrup to taste. Mix well, then freeze.

To make the pavé sponge, sieve the cocoa powder and the icing sugar. Whip the eggs in a processor for 10 minutes and then fold in the cocoa and icing sugar. Place in a 35 cm x 20 cm x 4 cm baking tray and bake at 200°C/400°F/Gas Mark 6 for 10 minutes.

For the white chocolate mousse, warm the crème patissière and then melt the chocolate. Mix the two together, then fold in the semi-whipped cream. Leave in the fridge to set.

For the dark chocolate mousse, first melt the chocolate. Meanwhile, whisk the coffee onto the egg yolks until a sabayon is formed. Fold the sabayon into the chocolate and then fold in the cream. Leave in the fridge to set.

To make each pave, use an oval mould (7 cm in length, 4 cm in height and 4.5 cm at its widest point) to cut out an oval shape of sponge. Spoon the white chocolate mousse into the mould until just below half way. Place the sponge on top, then fill the remaining mould with dark chocolate mousse. Refrigerate for 10 minutes.

Now, remove the pavé from the mould and place in the centre of the plate. Arrange a ring of fresh raspberries around the pavé neatly. Place a scoop of raspberry sorbet on top and garnish with sprigs of mint.

 Canadian Framboise, Southbrook Farms

apple tart

ingredients

30 g (1 oz) puff pastry

75 g (2½ oz) green apples

25 g (¾ oz) caster sugar

25 g (¾ oz) demerara sugar

25 g (¾ oz) butter

60 ml (2 fl oz) caramel sauce

50 g (1¾ oz) vanilla ice cream

45 g (1½ oz) blackberries

SERVES 1

Roll out the puff pastry to a thickness of 3-4 mm. Cut out a circle 12-15 cm in diameter and cook in a hot oven (200°C/400°F/Gas Mark 6) until crisp.

Peel and core the apples, halve them and then slice them very thinly. Arrange them in a fan on the pastry and sprinkle with sugar. Hold the tart in your hand, put an upturned baking tray on top and then turn the tart upside down. Bake at 200°C/400°F/Gas Mark 6 for 5-10 minutes until caramelised.

Turn the right way up onto a plate and serve with the caramel sauce, fresh blackberries and vanilla ice cream.

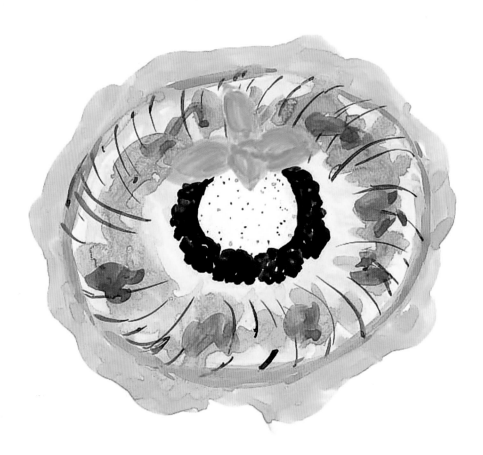

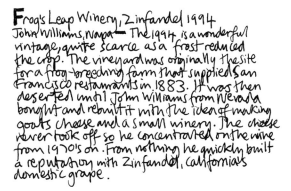

Frog's Leap Winery, Zinfandel 1994
John Williams, Napa — The 1994 is a wonderful
vintage, quite scarce as a frost reduced
the crop. The vineyard was originally the site
for a frog-breeding farm that supplied San
Francisco restaurants in 1883. It was then
deserted until John Williams from Nevada
bought and rebuilt it with the idea of making
goats cheese and a small winery. The cheese
never took off so he concentrated on the wine
from 1970's on. From nothing he quickly built
a reputation with Zinfandel, California's
domestic grape.

Petite Arvine 1995, Valais Canton, Cave Imesch
Sierre — A unique wine purely because it
is made with petite arvine grapes grown
only in this part of the world, Switzerland.
The initial taste is very close to a white Rhone.
Petite Arvine has a cleanness to its pure
fruit, and is best drunk young. It also has
a complexity from the soil, with chalky
limestone characteristics. Goes well with
the Mediterranean terrine, as it does not
have any oak, so respects every flavour
of the ingredients. There is a great freshness.

Canadian Framboise, Southbrook Farms
— A dessert wine bursting with the intense
fresh fruit flavour of ripe raspberries. The
wine is produced in much the same way
as port and has a concentrated fruit flavour
that does not finish with a cloying sweetness.
Raspberries from the farm are partially
fermented, and then the mixture is
fortified with pure grape brandy to bring
the finished strength up to about 14%.
This process ensures all the qualities
of the fresh berries are retained.
Excellent with chocolate desserts + ice cream.

Pic-Saint-Loup, 1996, Domaine de l'Hortus,
Jean Orliac — This red wine composed of
Syrah, Cinsault and Carignan grapes made
by a genius winemaker to the north of
Montpellier, now reputed to have made one
of the finest wines in the south. Fine deep
colour, perfumed nose with a hints of 'Garrigue'
(Provencal Herbs) Beautifully balanced with
silky ripe tannins and red fruits.

michel roux

An early memory I have of The Waterside Inn is of going for a trip down the river in the inn's electric launch. One of the waiters had been given the job of captaining the vessel and returning me safely. He had had some training, but could not be classed as skilled. On our return I saw Michel Roux waiting on the edge of the jetty, confident that we were all about to witness another faultless mooring – he even waved. I noticed that the waiter was not looking as calm and was, in fact, starting to fight with the strong current of the Thames flowing seaward. Even I could tell that the angle was wrong and, if we continued in the same direction, the launch would hit the jetty head on, knock Michel Roux into the water and probably do some structural damage to The Waterside Inn – Michel kept on smiling and waved again. I closed my eyes. When I opened them again, another waiter was holding on to a rope and the launch was manoeuvring safely to the jetty's side. Michel's composure, his never making a drama when problems arise, is perhaps a reflection of his training in the great private houses of France, where tact and good manners go hand in hand with demanding situations. It is a pity that most of these houses are disappearing as some of the younger contemporary chefs might benefit from such a discipline and curb the tendency to get a little carried away with their own emotions when something upsets the boat.

Michel Roux started winning prizes very early on in his career, but perhaps his 'personal best' is the Meilleur Ouvrier de France en Pâtisserie, one of France's highest professional awards of recognition and coveted in the same way as the Oscar is in Hollywood. How did a small boy from Charolles in Saône-et-Loire

achieve such success? It started when Michel and his brother, Albert, were influenced by the cooking of their mother, who always had something delicious on the stove in the kitchen. It is not surprising that Albert and Michel Roux soon developed their own fascination with food and, each in his own right, went on to become a far-reaching influence on modern cooking. When he was fourteen, Michel Roux went to the Pâtisserie Loyal in Paris to begin a three-year apprenticeship before going to work for the British Embassy in Paris as a commis patissier. After finishing at the Embassy, he gained his first experience of the detailed cuisine of a large aristocratic house when he did a year as commis with Mlle Cécile de Rothchild. On this occasion he did not stay long, having to do his military service. In the sixties, the decade when most of the world was 'tuning in and dropping out', Michel returned to the strict kitchens of the Rothchilds for six

more years. Indeed, he was the youngest head chef ever employed there. Although the management was precise, the wealth of the house gave him the chance to experiment without financial constraints. There is the well-documented story of his once preparing a garnish – a whole kilo of truffles in champagne! Other times, simple meals were requested at a moment's notice, but still prepared with the attention to detail as if they were banquets for a state visit. Life was always interesting and Michel had the opportunity to travel abroad with the family and improvise with ingredients bought from foreign markets. He has never forgotten all he learnt in the great private house, where cooking was akin to a liberal art.

In 1967, Michel decided to join Albert in starting their own restaurant, the first in Europe to introduce a high-class menu of twenty to twenty-five dishes and offer the same standards publicly as those of the aristocratic private houses. They chose London as the location and a name straight out of Victor Hugo's *Les Miserables*: Gavroche. Gavroche was the young street urchin or Paris *gamin*, who fought from the streets at the Paris barricades. The brothers felt a little like street fighters as they took on London, although ironically, from the earlier days, their guests were princesses, lords and show business stars. After a few years they had added Le Poulbot and Le Gamin to their enterprise. They found that Le Poulbot, in Cheapside, was busy every lunchtime with diners from the City and Le Gavroche was busy six nights a week, but they had nothing during the weekend – until Roux Restaurants' Director, François Merlozzi, found The Waterside Inn at Bray, Berkshire, in the early seventies. At the time it was a small pub with very little going for it apart from the riverside location. The Rouxs had the vision. 'We had the best restaurant in London,' Michel told me, 'and we were going to make the Waterside into the best restaurant in the country.'

The Waterside Inn opened in 1972 and achieved its first Michelin star in the same year. In 1974 it had a second, in 1985 the third. In the beginning, both Michel and Albert ran The Waterside Inn, but eventually they realised they needed their own space and it made sense for Albert to take charge of Le Gavroche and for Michel to concentrate on developing the restaurant and hotel at Bray. It was certainly a challenge, as Michel points out. 'Cooking in England was completely different twenty years ago: the food served was a mockery. With the top country house hotels they often had good accommodation, but average food. Now the standard is very high, in restaurants and hotels.'

In 1990 with a staff of thirty, Michel bought an adjacent house and turned what was a pokey rambling cottage into an elegant spacious private dining room. In 1992, in the middle of the recession, he managed to secure the freehold of The Waterside Inn. 'I believe in securing your position when there is a downward turn in the economy.' He added nine guest bedrooms to meet the demands of his clients. The two new projects took the staff total to forty. 'Obviously, it will take time to recover the cost of refurbishment and staff investment, but it's well on the way.' He smiled, a glint in his soft grey-blue eyes. 'Paying back the loan takes longer than signing the piece of paper.'

Most of The Waterside Inn's guests are regular, British, many from London though the summer months see people visiting from all parts of the world. When it is warm, the plate glass windows are opened and diners can

Michel Roux's kitchen

The Waterside Inn

feel that they are right on the banks of the river, soothed by sweeping willow trees whose slender branches continually dance. Michel insists on perfection and the inn for the last twenty-two years has been a member of the prestigious *Relais Gourmand,* the fine restaurant guide itself part of Relais & Chateaux, the company that only awards its exclusive mark to the few hotels and restaurants in the top band for quality. Michel freely admits to being extremely demanding and critical, but customers expect the food and the service to live up to the reputation. The guests themselves sometimes let themselves go a little: on one occasion, the manager, Diego, found a topless lady sitting in the red gazebo, obviously feeling the effects of a particularly hot summer or perhaps too much wine over lunch. When he asked if she was all right, without saying a word she stripped off completely and jumped naked into the river. Two of the female staff were waiting with linen tablecloths when the lady decided to get out – again, the right course of action with the minimum of fuss.

Michel now has his own club called the Michel Roux Club. He invites certain regulars to join and then to go abroad with him to various vineyards and wineries, visiting some great houses in Bordeaux and Burgundy, and to appreciate good food, good wine and good company. Some members are included in the cookery school he runs for three weeks of the year.

The head chef, Russell Holborn, is fully British trained and follows on from Mark Dodson, who moved onto Clivedon House. Keeping with the French great house tradition, however, it is Michel's son Alain, who after many years at The Waterside is now chef patron with Michel stepping out of the kitchen to concentrate on running the business. Alain has worked at The Waterside Inn for five years, and previously worked for seven years in numerous two and three Michelin-starred restaurants in France.

Michel Roux's first love is for the dessert, made clear in his 'My Secret Obsession' written in his book *Desserts: a Lifelong Passion:*

I catch myself smiling at her, a discreet furtive smile which I have secretly harboured for longer than I can remember. I felt its first feeble flickerings in adolescence; over the years it has heated into an incandescent furnace.

Ours is a faithful relationship, pure and bottomless, which cannot easily be expressed in words. It has deepened over many years through the senses: touch, sight, smell and even hearing. I rarely speak to her, but communicate only by vague movements of my lips, almost

like the first outline of a kiss.
I reinvent and recreate her every day, using
simple ingredients. Inspired by my thoughts,
my fingers model and caress her, gently dress
her, apply a hint of makeup with the touch of a
piping cone, and ornament her hair with a
sugar rose. Her beauty takes my breath away;
she thrills me and fills me with admiration.

Roux Diners' Club has its own scholarship system in place which, jointly with Michel Roux, sponsors one chef a year to go abroad and gain invaluable experience. The system teaches chefs to be independent, which Michel thinks is crucial. 'In any profession, cooking, golf, politics, those who stay at the top for a long time are the ones who are doing it for themselves. I cook for myself, what I like.'

Most of all he prefers the cooking of his talented Australian wife Robyn, who is in charge of their kitchen at home. Other times they escape to their house and vineyard near St Tropez where Michel gets a lot of pleasure going to market and buying a little food just to enjoy eating simply. He walks, shoots and plays golf, but not that often – finding a course is not a problem (Wentworth is not far away); finding the time it takes to play eighteen holes is! And there are, of course, Michel Roux's consultancies, for example advising British Airways on their first-class in-flight menus, and his record as one of the most successful cookery authors with seven books to his credit – at last count *Roux Brothers on Pâtisserie* had sold almost 250,000 copies.

The Waterside Inn and the surrounding area provides quite a natural canvas for the artist to use, whether it be the duck battalions that storm the terraces at four in the afternoon, the old lock gates further up the river, or the colourful barges that moor up at the jetty when parties come for dinner at night, left with lanterns burning in the windows as guiding lights for the journey home. At the restaurant itself, the gastronomic experience is as one would expect from a gourmet chef not only at the top of his profession, but something of an industry icon.

caneton challandais rôti à la lie de vin

ingredients

2 x 2.4 kg (5¼ lb) Challandais ducks

salt and pepper.

For the Purée of Spinach

200 g (7 oz) spinach, blanched and well drained

50 g (1¾ oz) butter

1 small tsp anchovy purée

50 g (1¾ oz) olives, diced

salt, pepper and nutmeg

For the Sauce

300 ml (½ pt) duck stock

6 large olives, stoned and chopped roughly

1 small tsp anchovy purée

4 drops bitter almond essence

40 g (1½ oz) butter

100 ml (3 fl oz) red wine

SERVES 4

Season the duck with salt and pepper inside and out. Put into a roasting tray, breast upwards. Roast in a very hot oven at 260°C/500°F/Gas Mark 10 for approximately 14 minutes until skin is light brown in colour. Remove the duck from the oven and turn upside down so that the blood and juices stay in the breast. Leave to cool by half.

Meanwhile, make the spinach purée and sauce. For the purée, melt the butter in a small pan. In a mixer, chop the spinach and the anchovy paste until smooth, then add the butter and seasoning. Now heat the purée in a small pan and keep in a warm place.

To make the sauce, put all the ingredients apart from the butter in a pan. Put on the heat and leave to simmer until the flavours infuse and the sauce lightly covers the back of a spoon. Now whisk in the butter (once the butter has been added, do not re-boil the sauce). Pass the sauce through a fine chinois and set aside. Re-heat gently when ready to use.

When the duck is half cool, remove the breasts and slice them evenly into 6 slices. Put onto a small flat pan and reheat under a grill until the skin is crisp and the duck flesh is pink. To serve, place a large spoon of spinach purée onto each plate. Using the back of the spoon, mould the purée into the shape of the duck breast and then place the reheated duck breast on top of it. Sprinkle the olives on top (for presentation) and pour the sauce around.

 Château Lanessan 1990

darne de turbotin grillée avec sauce ciboulette

ingredients

4 x 200 g (7 oz) skinned turbot steaks, cut on the bone from the centre of the fillet

1 tbs olive oil

1 large potato, sliced

salt and pepper

For the Sauce Ciboulette

250 ml (8 fl oz) olive oil

25 g (¾ oz) chives, snipped

SERVES 4

First make the sauce ciboulette. In a saucepan, heat the oil to about 80°C, add the chives and cover the pan. Immediately turn off the heat and leave the oil to cool. Once cold, whizz in a blender for 30 seconds, then pass the oil through a wire-mesh conical sieve, pour into a bottle and cork it. The oil will keep like this for several days.

Brush the prepared steaks of turbot with the olive oil and grill lightly, marking a criss cross pattern on both sides. Put each steak onto a slice of potato and onto a roasting tray (the potato will stop the steak sticking) and season with salt and pepper. Cook in a hot oven (240°C/475°F/Gas Mark 9) for about 5-7 minutes until cooked to your liking. Serve with a little of the chive oil drizzled over it.

 Riesling 'Grand Cru Furstentum' 1995

larmes de chocolat, mousse ivoirine et griottines

ingredients

250 g (9 oz) bitter couverture

72 griottines (small cherries in eau-de-vie syrup)

250 ml (9 fl oz) eau-de-vie syrup from the griottines, reduced by one-third over a low heat

6 sprigs mint

For the White Chocolate Mousse

200 g (7 oz) white cooking chocolate, chopped

50 g (2 oz) butter, melted

450 ml (16 fl oz) whipping cream

100 g (3½ oz) egg whites

75 g (3 oz) caster sugar

SERVES 6

First make the white chocolate mousse. Make an Italian meringue from the egg whites and sugar. Heat the white chocolate in a bain-marie to 40°C/104°F, stirring occasionally. Whip the cream to a ribbon consistency and fold a third of it into the chocolate with a whisk, then fold in the meringue. Finally, fold in the rest of the cream until the mousse is perfectly blended. Refrigerate until needed.

Now temper the couverture. To do this you will need a chocolate warmer and a chocolate thermometer. Chop the chocolate with a heavy knife and melt it in the chocolate warmer at 50-55°C/122-131°F. Pour about 80 per cent of the melted couverture onto a marble work surface and work it with a large palette knife, continuously bringing it up over itself until it cools to 26-27°C/78.8-80.6°F. Scrape the chocolate from the surface and mix it with the untempered couverture. Mix with a spatula and heat to 30-32°C/86-89.6°F.

Take 6 strips of acetate or rodoide 26 cm x 4.5 cm (10 in x 1½ in) and coat one side of each with the thinnest possible layer of couverture. As soon as it begins to set, pinch the two ends together in a loop and secure them with a paperclip to make a teardrop shape. Place the teardrops on a baking sheet lined with greaseproof paper and refrigerate for 30 minutes.

Use a piping bag to fill the teardrops one third full of white chocolate mousse. Arrange 8 griottines in each teardrop and then fill to the top with mousse and smooth the surface with a palette knife. Refrigerate until ready to serve.

To serve, remove the paperclips and plastic strips from the teardrops and put one on each plate. Use a piping cone to pipe some of the remaining couverture around the edge of the teardrop, and fill the top with the cold, reduced eau-de-vie. Arrange three griottines on each plate and one on each teardrop, and place a sprig of mint beside it. Serve extremely cold, with some chocolate sorbet if desired.

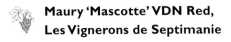 **Maury 'Mascotte' VDN Red,
Les Vignerons de Septimanie**

tarte des desmoiselles tatin

ingredients

6 medium dessert apples

juice of ½ lemon

120 g (4 oz) butter

200 g (7 oz) sugar

250 g (9 oz) puff pastry

SERVES 4

Preheat the oven to 220°C/425°F/Gas Mark 7. Peel, core and halve the apples, sprinkle them with lemon juice and reserve. Grease the base of round heatproof dish 26 cm (10 in) diameter and 7 cm (2 in) deep with the butter. Cover the the bottom of the pan with the sugar and then arrange the apples, rounded side down, on the bottom.

On a lightly floured surface, roll out the puff pastry into a circle about 3 mm (⅛ in) thick. Lay the pastry over the apples, allowing an overlap of about 2 cm (¾ in) all round. Trim off the excess with a sharp knife. Leave to rest in a cool place for at least 20 minutes.

To cook, put the dish over a fierce direct heat for 15-20 minutes, until the butter and sugar are bubbling and have become a deep amber colour. With a small palette knife, lift a little of the pastry away from the edges to ensure even cooking. Now cook in the preheated oven for 20 minutes until the pastry is risen and golden.

As soon as the tart is cooked, invert it quickly onto a round serving dish. The pastry will now be at the bottom of the plate, with the apples on top. If any have slipped, push them back into place with a small knife. Serve the tart piping hot.

 Château des Tours 1995 Sainte Croix du Mont

grandes tartelettes aux fruits, gratinés aux cinq épices

ingredients

420 g (14 oz) shortcrust pastry

flour for dusting

720 g (1½ lb) assorted fruits, chopped as necessary

1 quantity sabayon

½ tsp five spice powder

18 wild strawberries

6 small mint sprigs

For the Sabayon

3 egg yolks

65 g (2½ oz) caster sugar

50 ml (2 fl oz) water

75 ml (3 fl oz) raspberry eau-de-vie

SERVES 6

First, make the sabayon. Heat a bain-marie to 35°C-40°C (95°F-104°F). Combine all the ingredients and whisk in the bain-marie continuously for 10-12 minutes, making sure the water temperature does not exceed 90°C/194°F. It should swell to a ribbon consistency and be smooth and shiny.

On a lightly floured surface, roll out the pastry to a thickness of 2 mm (⅛ in). Cut out six circles with the pastry cutter and line the tartlet tins, lightly pinching up the edges of the pastry to make a border slightly bigger than the tins. Refrigerate for 10 minutes. Meanwhile, preheat the oven to 175°C/350°F/Gas Mark 4.

Prick the bottom of the pastry cases with a fork. Line with a circle of greaseproof paper and fill with dried beans. Bake for 10 minutes. Remove the beans and return the pastry cases to the oven for 1 minute to ensure that the insides are well cooked. Take them out of the oven and unmould on to a cooling rack.

Arrange the fruits in the tartlet cases, coat generously with two-thirds of the sabayon and glaze lightly under a hot grill for a few seconds. Immediately place the tartlets on warmed plates and pour the remaining sabayon in a ribbon around them. Arrange three wild strawberries and a small sprig of mint on each tartlet and serve at once.

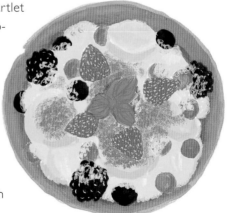

 Coteaux de Saumur 1990 Jean Claude Boudin

gordon ramsay

Gordon Ramsay's Kitchen has a certain characteristic pace to it, as does an international football game: fast, competitive and very intense. Gordon moves the fastest, 'at 150 mph' some might say. It's a formidable sight, unstoppable, the momentum of the stocky ex-Glasgow Rangers footballer in the role of chef patron within the confines of a kitchen. If, however, the image of a bull in a china shop springs to mind this would be quite wrong. Gordon Ramsay is without doubt a big chap, but as a chef he is more like a ballet dancer, always on his toes as he pirouettes round the pots and pans. Paradoxically, it usually takes a

few strong espressos to bring Gordon down after a busy service and, while I was painting there, it was during such coffee rituals that I tended to get the chance to talk with him.

I was first introduced to Gordon by his French manager, Jean Claude, who is more passionate about rugby than football. We made some personal predictions for the future of the game, as I prepared my brushes to paint a picture of the outside of the restaurant. After a few hours I was ready to disappear for a drink in the pub at the end of the road when Gordon appeared to see what this stranger with an easel was up to. He immediately warmed to the idea of the book

and, not long after, suggested that I design the plates for the Aubergine. I like to think we have an affinity with each other, having a mutual respect for creativity, both of us having worked hard to try and achieve our respective visions in life. Giving me some advice, Gordon told me how, if he complained of hardships in the early days, a friend would offer him words to the effect: you chose this path and you're responsible for it, nobody else.

In the Introduction to his first book, Gordon Ramsay cuts a strikingly different figure to many of the chefs on the Michelin circuit: 'I was not brought up with a food background. I did not pod beans at my grandmother's knee, gather forest mushrooms nor chase farmyard hens. My ambition was to play football for Glasgow Rangers which I set out to do in my late teens.' Ramsay does talk about his 'desire to strive for perfection'. His career was perhaps determined when he indulged in a spot of banqueting as part of a work-experience scheme. Before long, he found himself in a London kitchen producing food the quality of which he had not seen before. The kitchen was Harvey's, Marco Pierre White was the chef, and it gave Gordon Ramsay two formative years as a cook where he watched Marco's unique personal touch, experienced a sense of freedom and a growing confidence to express himself. After Harvey's he followed the traditional route for a fine culinary education and went to Le Gavroche and then to Paris to

work for Joël Robuchon and Guy Savoy. Gordon remembers the experience being so different to that of London, especially shopping for fresh ingredients in the rarefied atmosphere of the Bastille Market.

Gordon's own restaurant seemed to attract the favour of the gods and, with Fate on its side, developed quickly. The Aubergine received its first Michelin star within twelve months of opening and followed this with a string of awards, including Best Restaurant of the Year and Best New Chef; more important, it was fully booked at least a month ahead. London approved. It was with great pleasure that I gave Gordon a watercolour of some aubergines as a gift when he was awarded his second Michelin star.

Despite the constant danger of allowing success to run away with your integrity, Gordon is always conscious of continuing to improve and giving value for money. He believes a restaurant stands or falls on the efficiency of its kitchen and, drawing on football once more, he is very much the player manager, leading by example and taking responsibility not only for his own career, but for the ambitions and dreams of his staff as

well. Gordon Ramsay does not compromise and insists on flawless preparation, everything ready in advance, so the final creations are free-flowing natural expressions rather than a scramble of ingredients against the clock.

In 1998 Gordon's culinary questing at the age of 31, led him to set up his first independently owned restaurant, Gordon Ramsey, on the former site of La Tante Clare, near Chelsea's botanical gardens. But he does not see himself always in the kitchen. In 1999 he opened up Pétrus in the heart of Mayfair with his protégé Marcus Wareing as Chef Patron. Within seven months it had won its first Michelin star. He continued to expand in London and established Gordon Ramsey at Claridges in 2001. However it was in 2002 that he reached the pot of gold at the end of the rainbow, when his eponymously titled restaurant was awarded its third Michelin star. He has already undergone a transformation since I first met him, more commercially aware now, with his hand in food publishing and potential tie-ins with sporting events. Indeed, sport is never far from the big man's mind although, to all intents and purposes, playing football is a thing of the past. But Gordon has a growing interest in water sports and, whenever he can snatch some free time, enjoys water skiing and scuba diving with his wife, Tana, a school teacher. Gordon, Tana, and their three children now live in central London. But once they lived in an old converted school in Battersea which, at the beginning, must have been somewhat disorienting for Tana waking up to make breakfast and finding herself in a classroom. Converting a small disused football stadium, that would be the thing.

ravioli of lobster

ingredients

For the Ravioli

500 g (1 lb 2 oz) lobster meat, blanched and diced

100 g (3½ oz) fresh salmon fillet

½ tsp each of chopped basil, tarragon and chervil

20 ml (¾ fl oz) double cream

200 g (7 oz) pasta dough

For the Pasta Dough (Makes 800 g (1 lb 2 oz))

550 g (1 lb 4 oz) plain flour

generous pinch of salt

4 eggs

6 egg yolks

2 tbsp olive oil

SERVES 4

First make the pasta dough. Sift together the flour and salt and place in a food processor along with the eggs, yolks and oil. Process until the mixture starts to come together in coarse crumbs. Stop the machine and press a small amount of the mixture together with your fingers. The mixture should not crack, but if it does process it again for a few seconds. Tip the mixture out onto a board and knead well until you have a smooth, firm ball of dough. It should feel soft but not sticky. Wrap the dough in cling film and allow to rest for an hour or two.

Dice half the salmon to the same size as the lobster. In a food processor, blend the remaining salmon fillet to a smooth purée. Mix the purée, diced lobster, diced salmon, herbs and some seasoning. Divide the mixture into 4 little balls and roll them in your hands until dry. Chill until firm.

Take the 200 g (7 oz) pasta dough and roll it out thinly. Using a 10 cm (4 in) cutter, stamp out 8 circles. Place the 4 balls on 4 circles, and brush the edges with egg wash. Place a second circle on each and pinch the edges firmly together, stretching the dough if necessary and ensuring there are no air gaps or tears. Trim the excess edges with scissors. Cook in boiling water or lobster stock for 5 minutes.

Serve on a bed of basil puree and fresh tomato fondue. Sauce with a reduced lobster stock and a quenelle of olive purée.

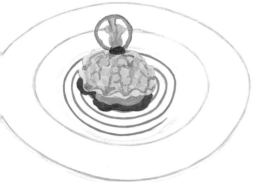

Mersault Premier Cru Genevrières 1983 Domaines des Comtes Lafon

red mullet with cous-cous

4 x 280 g (10 oz) red mullet, filleted, cleaned and boned

200 g (7 oz) cooked cous-cous

4 large scallops

24 small diamonds cut from aubergine skin

balsamic vinegar to marinate

For the Sauce

100 ml (3 fl oz) olive oil

50 ml (1½ fl oz) vegetable stock

10 g (¼ oz) tomato purée

5 g (⅛ oz) shallots, finely chopped

10 g (¾ oz) basil, chopped

1 tsp balsamic vinegar

SERVES 4

First prepare the sauce by adding all the ingredients together in a pan and warming very gently. Next, fry the aubergine diamonds and marinade them in the balsamic vinegar. Fry the red mullet and the scallops in separate pans. When they are nearly cooked, place some cous-cous in a ring in the centre of the plate and put some aubergine diamonds on top. Pour the sauce around the cous-cous and remove the ring. Place the red mullet and a scallop on top, and serve.

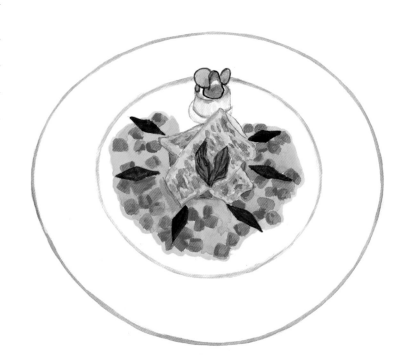

 Riesling Grand Cru Kitterlé 1991 Domaine Schlumberger

'Solanum melongena'

Aubergine is the fruit from a plant that is of the same genus as the potato and tomato. It is a perennial plant but is usually grown as an annual. They require much the same conditions as tomatoes warmth and a constant abundant irrigation. The flowers are star-shaped and a beautiful purple. The fruit varies in shape from round to oblong, and in colour from white to purple. They contain numerous seeds, so the fruit ought to be picked before they are allowed to become over-ripe.

Aubergine is the French name for the fruit, derived from the Catalan 'alberginia' which is itself a derivative of the Arabic 'al-badingan'. When the British sent the aubergine over to America it was white looking like an egg. Originating from India, where Sanskritic terms exist referring to the plant, the earliest records of cultivation are from China in the fifth century B.C. It was not widely cultivated in Europe until the sixteenth centuries when it was introduced by the Arabs who grew it in Spain.

It can be cooked in numerous ways, but cannot be eaten raw. Two classic recipes are 'Ratatouille' the vegetable stew from Provence and 'Imam Bayeldi' from Turkey where it is stuffed. The best time to buy them is from August to September when they are cheap and at their best with taut and shiny skins. The practice of salting aubergines grew out of two factors — the heavy moisture content that can make a dish watery, and a certain bitterness that is leeched by the salt along with the moisture. This bitterness has largely been bred out of modern aubergines. So salting is only normally necessary if you wish excess moisture to be removed.

roasted scallop salad

ingredients

12 large scallops, halved

80 g (2¾ oz) cauliflower purée

80 g (2¾ oz) raisin vinaigrette

100 g (3½ oz) mixed salad and dressing

chervil for garnish

SERVES 4

First make a purée of cauliflower by boiling the cauliflower and then liquidising it. Warm through and season. Make the raisin vinaigrette by liquidising equal amounts of raisin, capers and water. Pass through a fine chinois and warm. Dress the salad and arrange in the centre of the plate whilst quickly roasting the scallops in hot olive oil.

Arrange the cauliflower purée and vinaigrette around the salad and place the cooked scallops on top of the purée. Serve immediately.

 Pouilly Fumé 'Cuvée Majorum' 1989 Michel Redde et Fils

222

pot au feu of pigeon

ingredients

4 large Bresse pigeons

4 baby turnips

12 baby carrots

8 baby leeks

50 g (1¾ oz) green beans

50 g (1¾ oz) mange-tout

20 g (¾ oz) fresh peas

10 g (¼ oz) fresh broad beans

100 g (3½ oz) spinach, blanched

50 g (1¾ oz) celery

200 ml (7 fl oz) clear cep stock

1 l (1¾ pt) chicken stock

chopped truffle to garnish

chervil to garnish

SERVES 4

Prepare and cook all the baby vegetables to taste. Now clean the pigeons and poach them in simmering chicken stock for 7-9 minutes. Remove from the stock and then remove the breasts from the carcasses. If needed, reheat the breasts in the chicken stock.

To serve, place the blanched spinach in the a bowl with the vegetables and add two pigeon breasts. Cover the breasts with the hot cep stock and garnish with chopped truffle and chopped chervil.

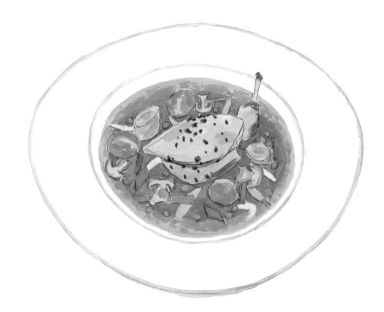

 **Pétrus 1978 Pomerol**

fillet of brill in civet sauce

ingredients

4 x 180 g (6½ oz) fillets of brill

200 g (7 oz) fine pomme purée

150 ml (5 fl oz) red wine sauce

2 bottles dark red wine

12 asparagus heads

12 baby leeks

50 g (1¾ oz) small girolles

50 g (1¾ oz) small leaf
spinach, blanched

50 g (1¾ oz) shallots, chopped

SERVES 4

First make the civet sauce. Sweat the shallots until soft, add half a bottle of wine, reduce to a syrup and then add the red wine sauce. Reduce to a coating consistency and keep warm.

Sauté the asparagus, leeks and girolles and keep warm.

Bring the remaining wine to the boil and poach the brill in it until just cooked. Place the pomme purée in the centre of a plate in a small ring. Reduce the ring and cover the purée with the blanched spinach leaves. Arrange the vegetables around the outside and place the brill on top of the purée. Season the civet sauce, spoon it over the fish and serve.

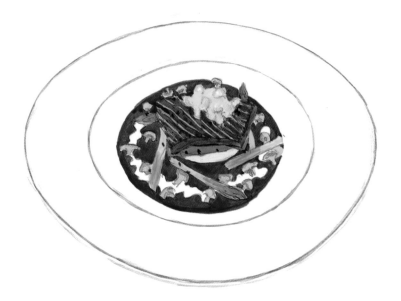

 Chambolle-Musigny, Domaine Dujac 1989

tatin of pears

ingredients

250 g (9 oz) puff pastry

10 firm pears (such as Packhams)

325 g (11 oz) caster sugar

50 g (2 oz) unsalted butter, diced

MAKES ONE 21cm (9 in) TART

Peel, quarter and core the pears, and then set aside. Put three-quarters of the sugar into a deep saucepan with about 4 tbsp water. Heat very slowly, stirring occasionally, until the sugar starts to dissolve. With a pot of water and a brush, wash down any sugar that clings to the side of the pan. When all the sugar has dissolved, stop stirring, raise the heat and boil until you have a rich, dark caramel. Immediately add the pear quarters (be aware that it might spit). Stir well, cover, and simmer for about 20 minutes until the pears are just soft. Leave to cool, then chill. Drain the pears, set aside, and discard the syrup.

Put the remaining sugar into a saucepan with 2 tbsp water. Dissolve and boil to a caramel as before. When it starts to smoke, whisk in the butter. When you have a smooth sauce, pour it into a 21 cm (9 in) flat tin or dish with a fixed base.

Roll out the pastry to a 23 cm (10 in) circle. Prick it well and put it in the fridge for about 10 minutes. Preheat the oven to 200°C/400°F/Gas Mark 6. Arrange the pears in the caramel sauce. Fit the pastry on top, tucking down the edges to hold the pears in place. Bake for 20-25 minutes or until the pastry is golden brown and crisp. Drain the excess juices off once during baking, leaving enough to keep the pears moist. Cool for 10 minutes then invert onto a plate and serve at room temperature.

 Château Rayne-Vigneau Premier Cru Classé Sauternes 1983

terrine of pink grapefruit, orange and passion fruit

ingredients

6 pink grapefruits

8 large seedless oranges

6 passion fruit

5 leaves gelatine

2 large bananas

125 g (4 oz) fresh strawberries

200 ml (7 fl oz) stock syrup

**For the Stock Syrup
(Makes 1.5 litres (2¼ pt))**

550 g (1¼ lb) granulated sugar

1 l (1¼ pt) cold water

grated zest of 1 lemon

SERVES 8-10

First make the stock syrup. Put the sugar, water and lemon zest into a heavy saucepan. Bring slowly to the boil, stirring occasionally. When all the granules of sugar have dissolved, boil for about 5 minutes. Cool and store in a sealed container until required.

Using a small serrated knife, cut the tops and bottoms off the citrus fruits. Cut away the remaining peel, removing with it all the membrane. Holding each fruit in your hand, and working over a bowl, cut out each of the segments leaving the inner membranes behind. Discard any stray pips. Place the segments on a clean tea towel to drain the juice and chill for 2 hours. Then place them on a fresh tea towel to drain further and chill for another hour.

Meanwhile, make a passion fruit syrup. Halve the passion fruits and squeeze their pulp and juice into a sieve placed over a bowl. Rub the pulp and seeds through using a wooden spoon. Mix the juice with the stock syrup.

Soak the gelatine in iced water until soft, remove and gently squeeze out the excess water. Heat half the passion fruit syrup until it boils. Remove from the heat and stir in the soaked gelatine until dissolved. Mix in the remainder of the passion fruit syrup, then strain the mixture through a sieve. Line a 1 kg (2 lb) loaf tin with cling film, leaving an overhang of about 13 cm (5 in) all around. Mix the syrup with the citrus fruit segments, then spoon about a third into the base of the loaf tin. Place a whole banana lengthways down one half of the tin; place half the strawberries down the other side. Spoon over more segments and syrup. Arrange the second banana lengthways down the opposite side from the first one. Add the remaining strawberries. Finish with the remaining segments and juice.

 Gewürztraminer Vendanbe Tardive, Leon Beyer 1989

Fold the overhanging cling film over the top. Chill overnight until firm. 15 minutes before serving, transfer it to the freezer. Then unfold the cling film from the top and invert onto a serving plate. Carefully remove all the cling film and serve in slices.

Pouilly-Fumé "Cuvée Majorum" 1989
Michel Redde et fils — The "cuvée
Majorum" is only vinified in the best
years using grapes from vieilles vignes
with an age of at least 35 years.
The wine is aged for at least two years
to allow the full bodied earthiness and
honeyed richness to develop. This Pouilly-
fumé is one of the top four in the appellation.

Pétrus 1978 Pomerol — The "Mozart" of
Pomerol. The magic lies in the soil
of the vineyard and its ancient vines,
average age is 40 years. The principle
of wine making at Pétrus is perfect
ripeness, then ruthless selection. As good
as its starry reputation. Sweet,
mouthfilling, round, lovely texture
and full of fruit. A wine matured all
for elegance and passion ideal with the pigeon.

Gewürztraminer Vendange Tardive 1989
Léon Beyer — The house of Léon Beyer
is one of the oldest of the region and are
owners of some of the best situated
vineyards, has maintained an unbroken
tradition as an outstanding wine
producer. This wine is late picked
Gewürztraminer and has resulted in
a wine with layers of richness and
long lingering flavour.

Meursault 1er Cru Genevrières 1983
Domaine des Comtes Lafon — Definitely
three star. Dominique Lafon is one of
the most talented wine makers in all
Burgundy. A good firm structured
white Burgundy. Vintage is memorably
one of the best. Hint of lime green
colour beautiful, flowering bouquet
with fabulous development in the glass
elegant, great length.

john burton-race

The ortolan bunting (*Emberiza hortulana*) is a small brownish bird once widely celebrated for the delicacy of its flesh. Before it became endangered as a species it used to be netted annually by the thousand. The birds were then put in dark rooms to keep them quiet and fattened on millet and oatmeal until they became little more than lumps of fat – in a previous era when the natural habitat was there for the taking this fat, apparently, was as tasty as that of the green turtle. After an ortolan was killed it was beheaded and had its crop removed before being cooked with the insides intact; sometimes it was drawn and stuffed with foie gras. You could always tell which restaurants served the ortolan because some live birds were kept in cages for the diner to see.

John Burton-Race started his former restaurant, L'Ortolan, with his friend, the late Sir David Napley. John chose the name after the almost extinct bird, still eaten illegally at some places, but never at L'Ortolan. John once gave me a blow by blow account. 'The way to eat it is with a triple-size napkin. You put it over your head and sit there in the middle of the restaurant. You have to do this because it is so revolting ... you eat the whole thing: bones, guts, everything – crunching all the time while eating – you don't want people to see you crunching on a whole baby bird, do you? Basically, it's hip and trendy.'

One never quite knows when to take John seriously, as his face seems to wear a permanent

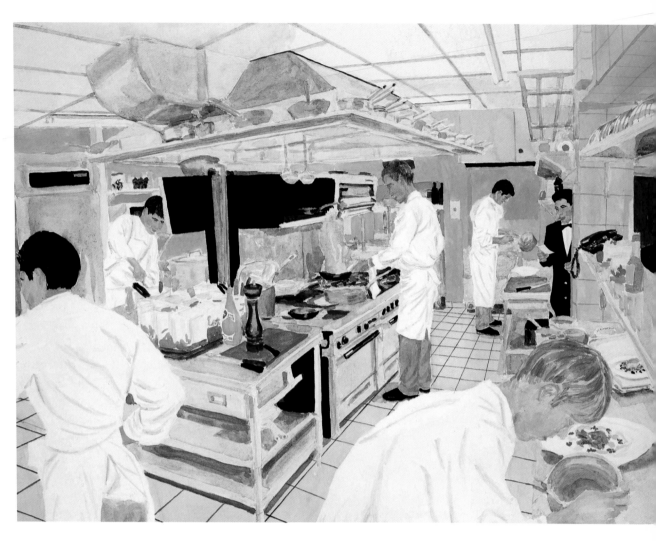

impish expression as if some form of mischief is at hand. He finds it amusing that he was once caught on one of those ubiquitous fly-on-the-wall documentaries when he was swearing at the sous chef and the sous chef was 'kicking the commis up the arse' (commis chefs are kitchen apprentices). Although, thanks to an enigmatic Maltese manager early on in his career, he rarely swears at people. 'This man was like a company hit man, sent into hotel trouble spots to clean them up … but he would do it in a very quiet way. One day I was on the vegetable service and

had a cheeky little waiter who came up and gave me some lip because I was late with the garnishes. I swore like a trooper and crowned him with whatever vegetables were in the pan. I was gently taken aside: "Look, you were quite right to crown the waiter, but I don't want to hear swearing in my kitchen." From that day on I used to just crown people quietly.'

I have always got on well with this self-confessed 'kitchen lunatic' and am used to his maniacal eyes, rarely fixing on any one thing for more than a few seconds, his fingers sometimes

rubbing on the skin of his forearms as if at any moment he might shout 'Out, damn spot'. Other times he looks terribly frail and I am reminded of the pacemaker he has fitted for a stress-related problem which means his heart could stop beating on the next breath. When he first blacked out a few years ago it frightened him because he did not expect it; now it frustrates him terribly as he is still ambitious. 'When you're younger money can slow you up. When your health slows you up it's terrible … it's like a chap who wants to walk across the room, but he's got no legs.'

At the time of his illness he was just getting over a very stressful divorce and for a year it was difficult for him to focus on anything properly other than the woman he fell in love with, who had four daughters. He admits that he was not himself, so the restaurant suffered at a time when he should have got his third Michelin star. When he came back he sacked twelve members of staff and set about improving the team. This reshuffle is indicative of John's habit, since an early age, of responding to problems quickly.

John Burton-Race was born in Singapore. 'When I was eleven my parents went off to work in Thailand. I lived with their friends … I used to see them three times a year in school holidays.'

John boarded at a public school in England and, in his own words, was quite good at art, liked English and history and was lazy in everything else, only doing the things he liked doing. When he went on to a sixth form college he lasted all of three weeks before putting down his books and dropping out. 'I remember my parents flew home and one of them gave me a hiding. I asked if I could take a year off and they said I'd had sixteen already.'

He liked to paint and he liked to eat. Art college was not an option as far as his father was concerned so, to get his parents off his back, John agreed to pursue catering as a career. They started dragging him round for interviews and he soon found himself at a four-star hotel in Winchester which he 'hated, absolutely hated'. It was the first time he had done any hard physical work, but he decided to grin and bear it to spite his parents. After about a year he decided he was actually enjoying it: it gave him freedom away from the 'Victorian' family home. He was still moonlighting as an artist and got asked to leave his digs for drawing murals all over the walls. 'They had a blood and guts theme ... Dali gone mad ... if Dali could be more mad than he already is. I worked hard for weeks on end and was very proud of them at the time.'

He compromised with the landlord and managed to extend his stay by agreeing to whitewash the walls before he left. He never did and, as far as he knows, the murals are still there. Next he went to London, moving about, gaining experience, working under different chefs – 'the long, hard slog'. Occasionally, he was asked to try hotel management, but never had any inclination for it. 'They probably asked me because I had a slightly below average

intelligence, whereas chefs, traditionally, are meant to have no intelligence.'

John has always enjoyed the cooking side of the business – he is excited by the creativity involved and fascinated by the science of why ingredients behave the way they do. He has an interest in the history of food, in its development across the world in all its different styles. Not surprisingly, having been brought up in the Far East, Asia has had an influence on his cooking.

Burton-Race first attracted attention in 1977 at the acclaimed hotel Chewton Glen in Hampshire. From here he went to La Sorbonne in Oxford, which employed Raymond Blanc. He eventually turned up as sous chef at Blanc's Le Manoir aux Quat' Saisons, then moved across to the less formal Le Petit Blanc as head chef. In 1986 he opened L'Ortolan, a red-brick former vicarage outside Reading dating from 1847 with a colonial-style conservatory. Here he began to transcend his reputation as a fine technician and was soon considered a master, creating dishes with a rare artistry – essentially regional French cuisine with plenty of fish and shellfish. He does not like silly food, 'pretty magazine food' as he calls it, and when he eats out himself he expects value for money and not to go home feeling as if he has been 'hit in the stomach by a wheelbarrow'. 'Nouvelle cuisine took ten years to disappear in this country, long after Europe had finished with it ... it was silly food which took a nice picture. The old traditional French way, with its rich sauces and heavy foods, is also fading because no one wants to die of a heart attack. Now the influence is more Mediterranean with olive oils and lighter food.'

At L'Ortolan he used strong flavours,

lightened textures wherever possible and changed the menu frequently – which he puts down to a low boredom threshold. He is more relaxed at the stove than away from it and expects a lot from himself and his brigade, never afraid that the nature of the work is all-consuming. When employing people to work in his restaurant John first looks for enthusiasm, followed closely by ambition. He is also wise in knowing that not everyone is cut out for the top of the profession and that every kitchen needs the so-called 'donkeys' to copy the work of the master. A top kitchen also needs the fresh influx of innovation, creative hands that will eventually outgrow the master – John considers an eighty/twenty split, respectively, a good balance. If he spots someone who has the potential and has learnt all he can, he will advise them to move on for their own good. He remembers one talented sous chef. 'If he would only "die a little bit more". With him there's a cut-off point … like a runner, you're knackered, but you've got to get to the end. This chef, he'll go nearly all the way, but at the last five hundred yards will stop – he needs to get over the pain barrier. It's the same as painting, you have to be slightly bonkers to overcome all the hardships … it's easy to jack it in. A few years ago I thought I was going mad because I was actually enjoying the pain.'

With his weak heart, John now has to adopt a different approach to his life, where ambition must be tempered with a certain amount of restraint. However, when I first met him, he was as eager as ever for his third Michelin star – 'I'm starving for it!' It was this ambition that took him to London in May 2000, where he opened John Burton-Race at The Landmark. He retains his two Michelin stars.

John no longer has any regrets about not pursuing art as a career – cooking has managed to satisfy the creative side of him. He is also a father and very much involved with his daughters and his son Charles. He does not think he will interfere in his children's path, but would like to 'get on to their wavelength' – he would certainly encourage them towards anything 'arty', though he would not advise them to enter the world of cooking. Like many chefs, John does find time to fish, both freshwater and sea, and likes nothing more than to be out on a boat at sea. He is keen with a shot-gun and says he has been brought into a farmer's syndicate as 'chief thug'. He has a passion for motor cars and used to be sponsored to race a Porsche 968 Club Sports at various circuits, including Silverstone and Goodwood. When I first met him he drove a hard price for some of my original works because he wanted to 'hold on to the Porsche'. Now his life insurance policy won't allow him to tear round the track, so he has calmed down and bought himself a 'family' Jaguar V8. As for the future, he says he is not as weird and wonderful as he used to be – 'if, indeed, I was weird and wonderful, certainly weird' – but has kept his curiosity and is always looking to develop the next interesting texture, to create that rare taste.

ravioli wild mushroom

ingredients

2 shallots, finely chopped

1 clove garlic, sliced

42 g (1½ oz) wild mushrooms

6 spears asparagus

1 tsp truffle paste

a little truffle oil

For the Rye Ravioli
(this will make sufficient for
about 10 raviolis)

450 g (1 lb) white pasta flour

18 egg yolks

100 g (3½ oz) rye flour

For the Asparagus Coulis

3 bunches green asparagus, chopped finely

1 large leek, chopped finely

1 medium onion, diced

2 cloves garlic, sliced

1 sprig thyme

1 bay leaf

500 ml (17 fl oz) chicken stock

20 g (¾ oz) butter

1 bunch baby spinach leaves

1 bunch chervil stalks

salt and pepper

SERVES I

Heat a little oil in a heavy saucepan and add the mushrooms, shallots and garlic. Season. Sauté, then leave to cool.

To make the ravioli base, mix the flour and egg yolks until smooth. Add the rye flour and mix in. Take 225 g (½ lb) of the mix and roll it as thin as possible on a pasta machine. Cut a square 12 cm diameter.

Add the truffle paste to the mushroom mix, then spoon the mix on to the ravioli. Dampen the edges, then cut a piece of the pasta dough slightly larger than the base. Dampen the edges, then place over the mushrooms. Seal the edges, making sure there are no air bubbles, and cut off any excess pasta. Leave to rest in the fridge for 30 minutes.

Meanwhile, make the asparagus coulis. Melt the butter in a stainless steel pan and sweat the onion and garlic. Add the asparagus, thyme and bay leaf and sweat, making sure the asparagus does not lose its colour. Add the chicken stock, bring to the boil and then add the spinach leaves. Liquidise in a blender and pass through a fine chinois.

To cook the ravioli, simmer for 3-4 minutes, then serve with the coulis poured around and with some asparagus stalks.

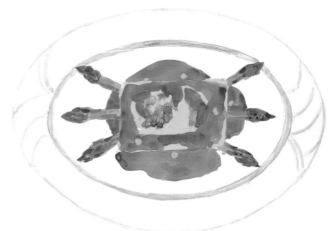

 1995 Pinot Gris Domaine Materne Hoegelin, Alsace

'Mullus surmuletus'

Red Mullet are mainly migrating fish that come inshore on the south and south-west coasts of Britain from May to September from warmer southern waters. It grows to a maximum size of about 3 lbs in weight and the main fishing grounds are in the Mediterranean. Mostly in the past the french would cook it without gutting in a similar way to woodcocks and therefore sometimes called it "bécasse de mer" – sea woodcock. The liver is prized and often used in an accompanying sauce. The taste of red mullet is very distinctive and can be strong depending on the ground the fish has been feeding on. They cook well grilled, score the skin first. It was much sought after by the Romans, one of the more gastronomic emperors, Claudius, once paid a sum of money equal to €100 by modern standards for a single fish.
   There are few more beautiful sights than seeing a shoal of red mullet in the clear turquoise blue waters off Cornwall.

fillets of red mullet, layered between slices of crisp aubergine and courgette

ingredients

2 small fillets of red mullet

100 ml (3 fl oz) fish stock

2 ladles tomato coulis

tapinade of black olives

40 g (1½ oz) baking powder

200 g (7 oz) cornflour

300 g (10 oz) plain flour

a pinch of salt

280 ml (½ pt) cream

1 courgette, cut into strips ½ in thick

1 aubergine, cut into strips ½ in thick

a few tomato petals (tomatoes cut in half)

SERVES 2

Make a batter by mixing the baking flour, cornflour, plain flour, salt and cream until smooth. Dip the courgettes in the batter mix then deep fry at 190°C/375°F until golden brown. Repeat this process with the aubergine. Place the vegetables on some kitchen paper to strain off the excess oil.

Heat the fish stock in a pan and cook the mullet in it for 2-3 minutes. Finish the fish under a grill to give a slight shine.

To serve, spoon some tomato coulis onto an oval plate. Add one layer of aubergine. Put two tomato petals on top. Add a fillet of red mullet, then a layer of courgette. Now add some more tomato petals, a final layer of courgette, and place a basil leaf on top. Spoon a little olive tapenade around.

quail épices

ingredients

10 prepared quails

For the Marinade

juice of 10 oranges

juice of 10 limes

4 tbsp brown sugar

2 tbsp desiccated coconut

1 juice fresh coconut milk

4 large tbsp curry paste

3 large tbsp curry powder

1 stem of ginger, chopped

2 small hot chillies, de-seeded and chopped

350 g (12 oz) olive oil

3 sprigs fresh coriander

200 g (7 oz) sweet soya sauce

200 g (7 oz) dark soya sauce

For the Curry Sauce

2 handfuls onions, carrots, leeks, all diced

1 gallon chicken stock

3 tbsp curry paste

3 tbsp curry powder

2 tbsp redcurrant jelly

1 head of garlic, cut in half

2 sprigs thyme

1 bay leaf

SERVES 4-5 AS A MAIN COURSE, 10 AS A STARTER

Prick the quails with a sewing needle so that they will absorb the marinade. Mix all the marinade ingredients and put in a bowl with the quails. Cover with clingfilm and leave for at least 24 hours.

When the quails have finished marinating, remove them and chop them small. Heat a little oil in a pan, then colour them until they are light brown. Add the diced vegetables and again colour until golden brown. In another pan, heat the chicken stock and then add the curry powder, curry paste and redcurrant jelly.

Add the chicken stock to the bones and vegetables. Add the garlic, thyme and bay leaf, bring to the boil and skim off any scum. Leave to simmer for 1-2 hours.

Strain the stock through a fine chinois and leave it to settle in the fridge for at least 24 hours. Now take off any fat from the surface and put the remaining stock in a reducing pan. Bring to the boil and skim off any scum. Reduce the stock by half, then pass through a muslin.

Serve with rice, peanuts and spring onions. If the sauce is too rich for your taste, add a little cream.

ravioli of passion fruit

ingredients

For the Pasta Dough

25 g (¾ oz) pork fat

a pinch of salt

150 g (5 oz) pasta flour

55 g (2 oz) water

For the Passion Fruit Curd

75 g (2 oz) sugar

100 g (3½ oz) passion fruit juice

50 g (1¾ oz) butter

2 large eggs

seeds of 2 passion fruits

juice of 2 oranges

For the Orange Sauce

80 g (3 oz) sugar

4 oranges

40 g (1½ oz) butter, cold and diced

seeds of 1 passion fruit

SERVES 4

First make the pasta. Place the pork fat into a mixer and blend for about 1 minute until it is soft and smooth. Pass through a fine sieve. Put the fat in a bowl with the salt and flour and rub them together until they are mixed well. Slowly incorporate the water, working the dough well and, when all the liquid has been added, remove from the bowl and work the dough on a work surface until smooth. Wrap in cling film and refrigerate for an hour.

To make the passion fruit curd, place the passion fruit juice, orange juice, butter and sugar in a saucepan, melt and slowly bring to the boil. Meanwhile, whisk the eggs thoroughly in a bowl, and have ready a sieve and bowl through which to pass the curd when it is cooked. When the mix has boiled, add the eggs slowly, whisking them in continuously. Bring the curd to the boil for 1 minute, pass through the sieve and set aside.

Now prepare the sauce. Put the sugar in a small pan and warm it gently. Add the juice of the oranges, boil and skim off any scum that might be on the surface, and then reduce it so that it becomes of a slightly thicker consistency. Remove from the heat and whisk in the cold butter and the passion fruit seeds.

When you are ready to make the raviolis, work the dough so that it is flat and can easily go through a pasta machine. Roll the pasta until it is 3 mm thick, cut into four, put each piece on top of each other, turn by 90 degrees and roll again. Repeat this process 4 times.

Now put the dough through a pasta machine so that it is approximately 14 cm wide and 1¼ cm thick. Cut into two pieces, ensuring one is larger than the other. Cut both pieces into 4 triangles and keep them under clingfilm so that they don't dry out. Place one of the smaller pieces on some silicone paper and, using a piping bag, pipe some curd into the centre, leaving 2 cm around the edge of the pasta and using no more than a quarter of the mix. Make a little indentation into the top of the

 1994 Pacherenc du Vic Bilh 'Vendemiaire' Alain Brumot

curd, place a few passion fruit seeds in it, and then replace the curd you used to make the hole. Dampen the pasta round the curd, and carefully place one of the larger pieces over it. Seal the edge of the curd with your fingers, and then cut off any excess pasta, making sure that you leave a I cm lip round the edge. Repeat the process for the other 3 raviolis.

To cook, boil a large pan of water and put the raviolis in with the silicone paper to stop them sticking together. Simmer for 6 minutes until they go translucent. Warm the orange sauce (but do not boil), remove the raviolis with a slotted spoon and serve on a plate with the orange sauce on top.

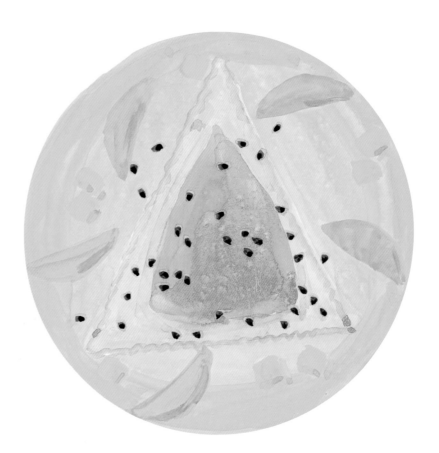

vanilla parfait

ingredients

1 egg yolk
45 g (1½ oz) caster sugar
1 leaf gelatine
125 g (4½ oz) whipping cream
1 vanilla pod

SERVES 1

Place into the bowl of an electric mixer the egg yolks and the seeds from the vanilla pod. Soften the gelatine in some cold water. Place the sugar in a small saucepan and saturate with water (do not use too much water, though, as this will make the syrup too weak). Bring to the boil and then pour it onto the egg yolks. Whisk continuously until light and fluffy.

Meanwhile, whisk the cream until it becomes thick. Put the softened gelatine in a pan with about 2 tbsp of the whipped cream. Heat gently to dissolve the gelatine and then mix very well. Combine this very well with the egg mixture, then gently fold in the remaining cream. Put the parfait in a mould and then freeze for 3 hours before serving.

 1989 Château d'Yquem Comtez de Lur Saluea

A plate of assorted desserts, of which the vanilla parfait is served as one

paul heathcote

P aul Heathcote is a robust individual, born and bred in Lancashire, a man who rolls with the punches and never gives up. He might have given up in 1990 when he watched his restaurant go up in flames, caused by a gas leak in the kitchen. It had only just opened, invested with all his savings and loan of £200,000 on eighteen per cent interest. He told me he has always been stubborn, eager to fight when someone or something tries to prevent him from doing what he wants. He came through

the catastrophe and, in 1994, Michelin awarded Heathcote two stars.

The Heathcote ancestry is not short of spirit. Paul's grandfather, Joe, was a coal pit miner who supplemented his income as a prize-fighter. Joe survived a pit accident, which broke his back, and two strokes. He started running marathons in his sixties. Now in his seventies, he is swimming every day and running round the borders of Bolton when the mood takes him. Joe's son, Ken (Paul's father) once

243

collected £25,000 for charity running from Land's End to John o' Groats. Paul used to be a keen runner, especially at Sharrow Bay in the Lake District where at nineteen he used to race round the shores of the lake before the breakfast service. At one point he thought fitness was his main strength and considered a career as a professional squash player, aspiring to the heights of Jonah Barrington. He would have liked to have played football for Bolton Wanderers, but is now content just to support them. He uses a football analogy to describe his naivety when he started cooking. 'I was in the Sunday League and had no idea that the Premiership even existed, let alone wanting to

play in it.' Perhaps a little less fit than he was, Paul now plays squash for Longridge and cricket for Chipping – he sees himself as a bowler rather than a batsman.

Paul Heathcote was born in Bolton in 1960 in a place where it is not wise to walk through the streets at night. Nothing is safe, even dogs – Paul's aunt is on her fifth. But it was at home that Paul discovered his passion and started to experiment with the oven, and often he cooked at his father's gym on Ladies' Nights. Boxing was never an option as Mrs Heathcote made sure her son would not emulate his grandfather. Paul tried to extend his interest to the school curriculum, but was quickly steered towards chemistry rather than domestic science. He finally managed to follow his ambition when, at sixteen, he left and went to Bolton College to do a three-year catering course.

Paul's first job was in Lockerbie, which was so bad he called home asking for advice. A lunch meeting with his father at a restaurant in the Lake District was, by pure chance, to show Paul his way forward. This was Sharrow Bay and the young Heathcote was so taken with it that he spent the next two years writing letters to Francis Coulson asking for a job. The persistence paid off and he spent two blissfully happy seasons there from 1982 to 1983. Paul

still had bigger plans, though, which meant he sacrificed the vistas and walkways that had so inspired Wordsworth. He took himself to London, to the fifty-strong brigade of the Connaught where a kitchen bully decided to single Paul out from day one. Paul could not be intimidated and stayed, learning many essential culinary disciplines from Michel Bourdin. In 1985 he changed his step again and went to Le Manoir aux Quat' Saisons, to the creative workshop which is the Raymond Blanc method. This period was to be the greatest influence on the way Heathcote cooks and he says he will always be indebted to Blanc. One of the things that impressed Paul about Raymond's

operation was how well the staff are treated and encouraged to develop – it means they stay longer. Paul now has the same working relationship with his own staff.

Paul Heathcote came home to Lancashire in 1987 when he was made head chef at the Broughton Park Hotel near Preston – it was here he met Gabbi, his future wife. He was now just three years away from his lifelong dream, his own restaurant, though he was not to know that fate would deal him a temporary cruel hand in the form of fire.

Heathcote's is still standing and there are four very successful Heathcote restaurants in Manchester, Leeds, Liverpool and Preston. The Simply Heathcote's in Manchester has a cookery school attached which is open all year round and caters for professionals and amateurs; the other is in Preston. Paul says that the brasserie clientèle are a little older than one would expect – what he describes as 'old yuppies'. 'They tend to have relieved themselves of children and paid off the

mortgage – they want to enjoy a few of the good things in life.' When Paul invited me to the Phillip Starck-designed Manchester location, Cliff Richard happened to be dining there, much to the delight of my female guest. Despite success and celebrity patronage all, however, is not how Paul would want, as he lost one of the stars from Heathcote's when the brasseries distracted him from his main work. He is tenacious and, no doubt, will fight until he has won back the prize. But Paul is not overly concerned with Michelin status; he does not cook for accolades, though he has collected his fair share. Paul believes fine dining is becoming less formal and more geared towards enjoyment, which is the way it ought to be. He thinks British cooking is now at its best and that the top chefs can compete with anyone in the world. He is quite friendly with most of the other master chefs; he spends time with Paul Rankin and shares his love of chilli oil. Paul also introduced the Chicken Man to London – but that's another story!

clear chilled tomato juice

YIELD 6 PTS

ingredients

50 g (1¾ oz) basil

100 g (3½ oz) chervil

1 shallot

3 sprigs of thyme

1 bunch of flat leaf parsley

1.25 kg (2 lb 12 oz) ripe tomatoes

125 ml (4 fl oz) white wine

After destalking and washing the tomatoes, place them in a container. Chop all the herbs and add these to the tomatoes together with the shallots, white wine and some seasoning. Using your hands, squeeze the tomatoes until all are crushed. Tie muslin over the container and hang upside down overnight with a fresh container underneath to catch the juices. Serve a small amount of the strained juice in a consomme cup garnished with chopped tomatoes, cooked vegetables and chervil, basil or tarragon.

 Lawson's Dry Hills Sauvignon Blanc 1997 (New Zealand)

black pudding

1 black pudding skin (stick size)

600 ml (1 pt) pig's blood

¼ onion, chopped and boiled until soft

50 g (2 oz) oats

1 sprig rosemary

1 sprig thyme

1 bay leaf, crushed

50 g (2 oz) sultanas

90 ml (3 fl oz) white wine vinegar

450 g (1 lb) veal or lamb sweetbreads

165 g (6 oz) foie gras (optional)

salt and pepper

Soak the sultanas in vinegar until all of it has been soaked up. Transfer to a pan, place over a low heat and continue to heat until most of the vinegar has evaporated, but don't allow the sultanas to caramelise. Take the sweetbreads and blanch them in boiling water for 1 minute before lifting out and peeling off the outer membrane. Dice into large pieces and fry in olive oil until golden brown. Dice the foie gras and put with the fried sweetbreads. Next take the pig's blood and, stirring continually, warm it over a bain-marie until it starts to thicken, finally passing through a sieve to remove any white membrane. Now mix the sultanas, sweetbreads and blood together. Crush the bay leaf and, with freshly picked sprigs of rosemary and thyme, add to the pudding mix and season with salt and pepper. Place the mix into a pudding skin and poach in a bain-marie at 82°C until the pudding has reached 75°C in the middle. Allow to cool, slice and grill with olive oil.

 Pinot Gris Reserve 1995, F. E. Trimbach, Alsace

skate wing on a bed of spinach

ingredients

1 large skate wing

20 cooked mussels

30 g (1 oz) capers

20 g (¼ oz) onions, blanched and diced

30 g (1 oz) gherkins, diced

1 plum tomato, peeled and diced

8 g (¼ oz) parsley, chopped

lemon juice

200 g (7 oz) spinach

1 clove garlic

20 g (¾ oz) butter

200 ml (6 fl oz) vegetable stock

1 tsp cream

125 g (4½ oz) butter, cold

SERVES 4

Portion the skate by removing the flesh from the bone and cutting into four – reserve the portions in the fridge. Reduce the stock by one half, add a drop of cream, the 125 g cold butter and season with salt and pepper and a little lemon juice. Fry the skate in a hot pan with a little oil. At the same time cook the spinach with the clove of garlic and chunk of butter. Season. Place the spinach in a bowl and, after seasoning with salt and a little lemon juice, rest the skate on top. Keep warm. Add the garnish to the sauce and heat without boiling. Spread the garnish and sauce round the skate and serve.

 Bouchard-Finlayson Sauvignon Blanc 1996 South Africa

rice pudding

ingredients

140 g (5 oz) pudding rice, soaked

1 l (1 pt 13 fl oz) milk

1 vanilla pod

70 ml (2 fl oz) hazelnut oil

4 eggs

125 g (4 oz) sugar

For the Caramel Ice Cream

250 ml (8 fl oz) milk

125 ml (4 fl oz) cream

5 egg yolks

175 g (6 oz) sugar

25 ml (1 fl oz) water

First make the ice cream. Boil the milk and cream. Cream 50 g (1¾ oz) of the sugar and the egg yolks, then pour the boiled milk onto the yolk mixture. Pour back into the pan and cook until the custard is thick enough to coat the back of a spoon. Now boil the water and the remaining sugar to make a dark caramel. Add 75 ml (2½ fl oz) cold water, then add the cool caramel to the custard and churn in an ice cream machine.

To make the rice pudding, place the rice, milk, vanilla pod and oil into a heavy pan and cook until tender. Cream together the eggs and sugar, bring the rice to a roaring boil and stir in the mixture. Leave to cool and then serve with the ice cream.

 Heggies Botrytis Riesling 1996 Eden Valley, Australia

hot apple crumble soufflé

ingredients

2 bramley apples

1 tbsp cornflour mixed with a little water

45 g (1½ oz) butter

90 g (3 oz) brown sugar

90 g (3 oz) plain flour

90 g (3 oz) ground almonds

4 egg whites

100 g (3½ oz) sugar

SERVES 2

Cut the apples just above half-way and scoop out all flesh, keeping the apple shells to one side. Place the flesh in a pan with a little water and cook until all the apple has turned into a fine pulp. Thicken with cornflour and hold the apple coulis to one side. Crumb the butter and flour, add the brown sugar and ground almonds, spread over a tray and bake in an oven until golden brown. Whisk the egg whites with sugar until a meringue forms. Take the apple coulis and make a paste with a little of the meringue before folding in the rest. Add a little of the crumble mix before filling the apple shells. Cover the tops with the remainder of the crumble and bake at 200°C/400°F/Gas Mark 6, for ten to twelve minutes until fully risen.

 Willi Opitz Pinot Gris Beerenauslese 1995, Austria

baked egg custard tart

SERVES 6-8

ingredients

12 egg yolks

65 g (2¼ oz) sugar

750 ml (1¼ pt) cream

250 ml (8 fl oz) milk

1 vanilla pod

3 tsp cornflour

10 drops rosewater essence

baked pastry case,
approximately 23 cm (9 in)
diameter (depending on depth)

Whisk the egg yolks with the sugar and vanilla. Boil the cream and milk and pour this onto the egg mixture. Pass through a sieve and skim. Pour into the pastry case and cook at a very low heat (about 95°C/200°F) for about 30 minutes.

Heathcote's assiette of desserts, of which the baked egg custard is served as one

'Cynara scolymus'

Artichoke is part of the thistle family and is a perennial, found in the wild but has been cultivated for thousands of years. Tends to need replanting every three or four years, due to the yield decreasing, from the young shoots that appear at the start of each growing season from the base of the plant. There are a few varieties, the most familiar culinarily being the globe artichoke. The part that is eaten is the flower bud, which is harvested young and tender with a tight head.

To cook, wash sitting pointed end down in a bowl of cold water so any dirt can fall out. Boil vigourously for 30-40 minutes leaving the lid off the saucepan otherwise the vegetable will take on a bitter flavour. They go well hot with lemon butter or hollandaise sauce and cold with vinaigrette dressing. Pull the leaves off one at a time, dip them in the sauce and scrape the flesh off between the teeth. Eventually one comes to the pale whitish/purplish centre leaves, which are discarded along with the fuzzy 'choke'. Reavealing the fat, fleshy base of the flower (fond). This prize part can be eaten with a knife and fork. The smaller heads picked at the end of the season can be preserved in oil by cutting in quaters lengthwise and boiling them in a mixture of water, white wine, salt and vinegar. Artichokes curiously alter the chemistry of the taste buds to make other foods taste sweeter.

marco pierre white

When I first contacted Marco in 1997 I must admit I was a little unsure what to expect. A fellow artist had described him as the Caravaggio of chefs. Here was a man who was something of a superstar, constantly courted by the many who fancied their chances of being allowed into his inner circle. So, I was more than a little surprised when he returned my call the same day and suggested that I meet him after lunch. We sat and had coffee in The Restaurant at the Hyde Park Hotel where he first won his third Michelin star, the first British-born chef to achieve this. Rather than talk about cooking

Marco decided to show me his collection of artworks. Once, he asked me if I knew a certain MP's son, Jonathan Yeo, who paints nudes – 'You ought to be doing that, Richard,' he suggested, 'rather than painting chefs in kitchens.'

Before he left, Marco's treasure at The Oak Room was a wonderful collection of animal bronzes, the work of sculptor Rembrandt Bugatti (1885-1916), brother of the more famous Eltore, the man behind the classic motorcar marque. Though rare, there are quite a few bronzes, including an elephant, lion, lioness and hippopotamus. I could tell how much Marco

he might ask very politely if he can ask a question during an intense debate – usually the others are silent while they wait for his probe. He used to drink endless cups of coffee, but this eventually caught up with him and he unfortunately developed an ulcer. When I was at The Oak Room he drank chamomile tea and was on a special diet; he never complained. In fact, I found it was I who became quite concerned for this larger-than-life personality chef. Concern, however, is the last thing Marco needs as he can certainly look after himself.

cares for them when one morning he excitedly showed me and everyone else present the new moose he had bought. The elephant is my favourite and for Marco's birthday I worked on a painting and presented it to him. Marco is also particularly fond of a series of eighteenth-century kitchen and chef paintings by Ribot and is always on the look out for more. When I suggested that I might paint him in his own kitchen he was a bit reluctant, thinking it too personal and preferring to keep my observations to the dining room and dishes. Later, when he came to understand me a little bit more, he seemed to warm to the idea.

When Marco was at The Oak Room in 1997 I spent four months beavering away in-between services to paint a watercolour of its interior – it is certainly one of the most opulent on the Michelin circuit. It was here that I saw something of the social side of Marco. Often he would receive people – friends, acquaintances and business contacts – in the large lounge just off the dining room. He loves to show people things, to inform, to instruct and usually pre-empts his guidance with the words 'my personal opinion'. Other times

White grew up in Yorkshire with his two older brothers, Graham and Clive, though his Italian mother decided to bolster his Latin heritage by calling him Marco. As a boy he loved the times he spent in Italy and the country is never far from his dreams. In England he was teased over his name and spent most of his school days fighting – his large size meant that the other boys soon came round to Marco's way of thinking. He started his career in Harrogate, at the Hotel St George: in his book, *White Heat*, Marco says 'I was sixteen and I didn't want to be a chef. I simply wanted freedom and a good time.' It was a few years later that he had his auspicious meeting with Albert Roux at Le Gavroche and was told that he would be welcome as an apprentice … if he cut his hair! Albert's recognition

of Marco's genius was confirmed when, at twenty-five and at Harvey's, Marco became the youngest chef ever to be awarded two Michelin stars.

The mature Marco we now know is undoubtedly a chef patron. He is the guiding light of numerous top London restaurants including an auspicious stint at the Café Royal with its ornate gold and red dining room. The Café Royal was established in 1865 and became an international mecca, famed for its cuisine and cosmopolitan atmosphere in which people such as Oscar Wilde

and Bernard Shaw would hold court. Wilde once said 'To get into society nowadays, all one has to do is either to feed people, amuse people or shock

people, that's all.' The original proprietor was one David Nichols Thevenon, later just Nichols, who jumped at his son-in-law's suggestion of putting his initial 'N' in a laurel wreath as a crest for the Café Royal. Nichols, a French Royalist, was not aware that his Bonapartist son-in-law had tricked him into championing Napoleon's name. Other concerns are Mirabelle – his old flagship with its ample kitchen and large brigade, Quo Vadis and L'Escargot, both integral features of London's Soho scene. Most recently, Mirabelle has become his flagship which, along with L'Escargot, has been awarded a Michelin star. This restaurant was originally at its height in the 1950s when it was converted into the most expensive Japanese dining room in the world. This was shipped back to Japan when Marco took over, though a Japanese private dining room still remains, with shark-skin leather on the pillars of the bar. Marco Pierre White has no plans to stop there. Despite the success and media attention he insists he is still learning and is yet to achieve his full potential. For this reason it is rare for Marco not to be in the kitchen during a service, though with his growing list of restaurants, unless he has become a mystic, he cannot be in more than one

place at once. Watching Marco cook is a unique experience as he prepares the food as if always for the first and last time, with total fascination, concentration and care. He describes his food with words such as 'sensuous' and 'feminine' and is well known for his need constantly to touch his food with his fingers. The more squeamish are sometimes put off by such intimate contact, but they might do well to remember the healthy curiosity most children have, for example, with the mixture left in a mother's cake bowl – what better judgement of taste? Marco Pierre White is, unquestionably, a man with aspirations, but where is it leading him? Perhaps the Salvador Dali quotation he chooses to print on his menu for The Oak Room might provide a clue:

At six I wanted to be a chef, at seven, Napoleon, and my ambitions have been growing ever since

tagliatelle of oysters

20 fresh oysters

225 g (8 oz) dark green cucumber

25 g (1 oz) butter

225 g (8 oz) fresh tagliatelle

2 tbsp caviar

fresh seaweed and/or rock salt

For the Sauce

4 shallots, finely chopped

75 ml (3 fl oz) white wine vinegar

225 g (8 oz) unsalted butter, cut into cubes

salt and freshly ground white pepper

lemon juice to taste

SERVES 4

First make the sauce. Put the shallots in a pan with the vinegar and bring to the boil. Continue to boil for a minute of two, then add a few drops of cold water and bring the mixture back to the boil. Remove the pan from the heat and, piece by piece, whisk in the butter, gently but quickly. Leave to infuse for 20 minutes, then season with salt, pepper and lemon juice. Pass through a muslin-lined sieve. Taste and adjust seasoning again. Warm through just before serving.

Now, peel and de-seed the cucumber and cut it into thin strips about 4 cm (1 in) long. Put in a pan with half the butter and just enough water to cover. Simmer until the cucumber is just tender. Drain, pat dry and keep warm.

Shell the oysters and retain their juices and the rounded shell. Thoroughly scrub the shells clean, place them in a small pan with enough water to cover and bring to the boil, to sterilise and warm them. Strain the oyster juices to remove any traces of shell. Place the juices in a small pan, with a little water if it seems it will be necessary just to cover the oysters. Bring to the boil, and then add the oysters. Poach gently over a low heat until they are just firm to the touch. Drain, pat dry and keep warm.

Warm the tagliatelle in just enough water to cover and the remaining butter, along with seasoning to taste. To serve, dress each plate with seaweed or rock salt, and then place 5 warm shells on each. Drain the tagliatelle and wind it round a fork to make a nest to settle inside each shell. Place an oyster on top and then cover with a few strips of cucumber. Spoon some sauce over the oysters and then place a few grains of caviar on top of each.

Pouilly-Fumé Silex 1995
Didier Dagueneau

roast saddle of rabbit, etuvée of asparagus and leeks with jus of rosemary

ingredients

1 saddle of rabbit

3 tbsp clarified butter

salt and freshly ground white pepper

200 ml (7 fl oz) chicken stock

25 g (1 oz) unsalted butter

1 tsp whipping cream

1 sprig fresh rosemary

For the Etuvée of Asparagus and Leeks

5 small asparagus spears

5 baby leeks

3 tbsp olive oil

chicken stock to cover

SERVES 2

First make the etuvée. Heat the olive oil in a large pan, and gently sweat off the asparagus and leeks for a few minutes without colouring. Add the stock barely to cover, and cook on a high heat until the stock and butter have virtually evaporated to a glaze and the vegetables are perfectly cooked.

Trim the saddle of rabbit, leaving it on the bone, and cut off the belly flaps. In an ovenproof pan, fry the saddle and belly in 2 tbsp of clarified butter until golden. Lift out the saddle, and arrange the belly pieces on the base of the pan. Replace the saddle on top of the belly and roast in the oven at 240°C/475°F/Gas Mark 9 for about 8 minutes. Leave to rest for 6 minutes.

Cut the belly pieces into very thin julliennes and fry in the fat remaining in the pan until very crisp. Drain well and keep warm. Remove the fat from the pan and add the stock. Stir, boil and reduce by half. Whisk in the butter, then the cream, and then leave the rosemary in it for a few minutes to infuse. To serve, pour the sauce around the saddle pieces, top them with the crisp belly, and arrange the asparagus and leeks as in the picture.

 Montrachet 1982

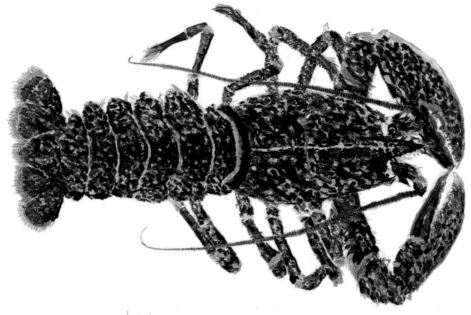

'Homarus gammarus'

Lobsters belong to a group known historically as the macrurans ('large tails'). They are very beautiful primitive creatures with a shell covered in purples and blues depending on the colours of its varying habitat. Particularly colourful living in clear water and near sand, they live under rocks or in holes, and are very adaptable On shipwrecks they often turn their claws a rust colour as camouflage. As an escape mechanism they can shed a claw which will grow back. They migrate inshore in the summer with the warm water to mate and feed; this is when they are at their cheapest and most plentiful in the markets. The European lobster is considered finer flavour than the American/Canadian ones which make up the shortfall in the market particularly in the winter. A lobster will moult its shell often in its early years as it grows, but as it gets older it will be about every two years. Ones with soft shells have recently moulted and ought to be left alone as they will be watery with less meat.

They are caught with baited pots, being carnivorous hunters and scavengers sometimes even cannibalistic given a chance. They mainly come out of their holes at night. When diving for them, you will often find a back entrance to their abodes. Place a pole in and tap their tails to coax them out. You then have to firmly grab the lobster from behind on its body, not an easy thing when its claws are facing you. They can swim very quickly backwards for about 20 mettes before tiring. You can at least fish selectively like this, the tail of the male narrows at the end whereas the females stays wide to be able to carry the eggs.

Lobsters do not have a brain, but a long nerve running down the length of them in the middle. To kill them you need to cut this either by cutting them in half length ways if you are grilling them or by inserting the point of a sharp knife in the cross on the shell behind the head and twisting. It is easy to over cook a lobster, small ones only need 5 minutes. Fresh lobsters will be quite active especially when splashed with water. They are delicious steamed and eaten cold with mayonnaise, new potatoes and salad.

lobster with its own vinaigrette

4 x 675 g (1 lb) fresh lobsters

15 g (½ oz) butter

48 very thin baby leeks, trimmed

160 ml (5 fl oz) olive oil

55 ml (2 fl oz) white wine vinegar

salt and freshly ground white pepper

For the Court-Bouillon (Makes about 1.75 l (3 pt)

3 leeks

1 carrot

1 stalk celery

4 shallots

3 onions

1 whole head of garlic

1.75 l (3 pt) cold water

1 leaf of bulb fennel

sprig of thyme

sprig of tarragon

a few stalks of parsley

8 peppercorns

20 g (¾ oz) salt

SERVES 4

First make the two stocks. For the jus d'homard, heat the oil in a large frying pan and add the lobster heads. Fry for about 2 minutes over a moderate heat, stirring well. Add the cognac and deglaze until all the liquid has evaporated. In a separate heavy pan, heat the remaining oil and fry the celery, carrot, shallots, leek and garlic until soft, and then add the contents of the first pan to it. Pour in the wine, bring to the boil and reduce by half. Add the fish stock and water and bring the mixture back to the boil. Add the spices, herbs and tomato purée, bring to the boil and simmer for 20 minutes. Sieve the contents of the pan and discard the solids. Pass 5 times through a muslin-lined sieve.

For the court-bouillon, coarsely chop all the vegetables and slice the garlic in half so that it halves each clove. Add enough cold water to cover and bring to the boil. Add all the remaining ingredients and simmer for 35 minutes. Pass the mixture through a sieve and discard the solids.

To make the sauce for this dish, reduce 250 ml (9 fl oz) of the jus d'homard by a third over a high heat. Whisk the oil and vinegar together and season, then finish with the butter. Mix the jus and the vinaigrette, and keep warm.

Now make a garnish by cooking the leeks in boiling salted water until just soft. Just before serving, you will need to reheat them in an emulsion of butter and water.

Separate the lobsters' tails and claws and reserve the heads for the garnish, if wished. In a large pan, bring enough court-bouillon to the boil to cover the lobsters. Poach them gently in it for 3 minutes. Drain and then carefully remove the flesh from the shells in whole pieces (1 tail and 2 claw pieces per lobster).

zest of 1 lemon

1 star anise

250 ml (9 fl oz) dry white wine

For the Jus d'Homard (Makes about 1.1 l (2 pt))

75 ml (3 fl oz) olive oil

4 x 675 g (1 lb) lobster heads

5 tbsp olive oil

2 tbsp cognac

½ stick celery, diced

½ small carrot, diced

3 shallots, finely sliced

white of 1 small leek, shredded

½ head garlic, sliced crosswise

400 ml (14 fl oz) dry white wine

1 l (1¾ pt) fish stock

300 ml (½ pt) water

1 star anise

10 pink peppercorns

sprig of thyme

2 large basil leaves

½ bay leaf

4 tbsp tomato purée

To serve, arrange 12 leeks on each of 4 warmed plates, with the white bases pointing outwards. Cut the lobster tails lengthways into 3 and fan these out over the beds of leeks. Place the 2 claws at 4 o' clock and 10 o' clock respectively, with the lobster heads between them if desired. Spoon the sauce over the lobster flesh. If desired, you can serve a ball of tagliatelle on a side plate.

 Châteauneuf du Pape Château Rayas White 1990

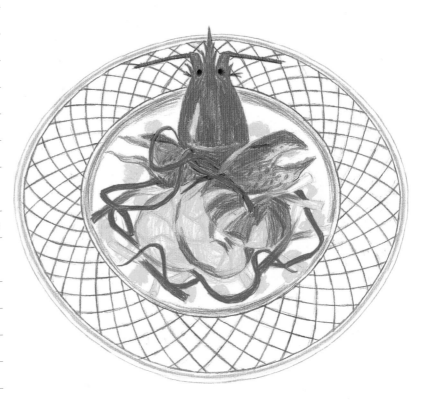

ballontine of salmon

ingredients

1 x 4.5-5.5 kg (10-12 lb) fresh salmon, filleted and skinned

2 bunches each of chervil, chives, tarragon, dill, flat leaf parsley, all finely chopped

1½ leaves bronze leaf gelatine

salt and cayenne pepper

milk and water for poaching

To Serve

keta eggs

fromage blanc

toasted brioche

Season the salmon with salt and cayenne pepper. Leave for 15 minutes and then dry with kitchen paper. Meanwhile, lay out 2 sheets of cling film so that they overlap each other by about a third and the total length is about 5 cm longer than the salmon. Lay another two sheets of cling film in exactly the same manner on top of the first two.

Place half the herbs on the cling film and press the skin side of one of the fillets of salmon onto the herbs. Place the gelatine on the salmon. Now place the other fillet, head to tail, on top of the bottom piece, skin side up. Coat with the remaining herbs. Roll tightly in the cling film and tie at both ends, being careful to exclude as much air as possible. Now tie the salmon at three equal intervals to retain the shape. Roll in a wet tea towel and tie as before.

Poach in a heavily seasoned liquor of half water and half milk for 3 minutes per pound at 70°C. Cool in the liquor for 1 hour, remove, cool and then refrigerate for 24 hours.

To serve, place a slice of ballontine just below the centre of the plate, with a quenelle of fromage blanc in the centre of the ballontine. Place the keta eggs on top and put the brioche just above the ballontine.

roast pineapple with vanilla

SERVES 4

First, take the vanilla pods and cut them into 1 in strips. Place them in a bowl and leave to dry somewhere warm. Now, make the sauce. This should preferably be done about 24 hours before roasting the pineapple. Place the sugar and vanilla pods in a large pan. Heat until the sugar forms quite a dark caramel. Add the chilli, banana and ginger. Then add the rum and finally the water. Leave to cool and then liquidise in a food processor. Pass through a sieve and leave.

When you are ready to roast the pineapple, remove the stalk and, with a serrated knife, peel the pineapple from top to bottom, trying to maintain the natural shape. Remove the core from the pineapple. Skewer rings of 6 dried vanilla pods the length of the pineapple. Place 2-3 ladles of the sauce into a high-sided pan, and then place the pineapple in it. Roast in an oven at 170°C/340°F/Gas Mark 4 for an hour and a half, basting every 15 minutes.

Serve with fromage blanc, ice cream and genoise (which is similar to victoria sponge, only made with butter).

 Château d'Yquem 1937

Pouilly-Fumé Silex 1995 Didier Dagueneau - Didier Dagueneau is the appellation's best winemaker. A maverick with 28 acres of vines, he was the first to ferment Pouilly-Fumé in oak barrels. The result is a rich wine made from 100% Sauvignon Blanc grape that is more like a white Burgundy in style.

Billecart-Salmon Rosé NV Champagne - From the small highly respected 'grande marque' this family firm founded in 1818 produces exquisite champagne respectful of the traditional composition of its 'cuvées', Billecart nonetheless uses modern vinification techniques which results in wine with floral aromas and delicate flavours. This subtle pale-salmon coloured Rosé is the flagship in their range. The result of a white vinification of the best crus of 40% Chardonnay, 40% Pinot Noir and 20% Pinot Meunier from their vineyards in Mareuil-sur-Aÿ.

Châteauneuf-du-Pape Chateau Rayas white 1990 - From an outstanding property the Reynaud family have 38 acres. This wine is made with old vines of Clairette giving a rich, nutty and full taste. It's hard to find and it's Gérard Depardieu's favourite.

Montrachet 1982 - For every wine lover, it is the best white Burgundy in the world. Only 3000 bottles produced a year and it is very persistent on the palate. In part from the site and soil, but also due to the vines being mean ly pruned, picked late and only the best used. Such economics only work for a vineyard whose wine is as good as sold before it is made, at almost any price.

richard bramble collection

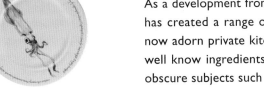

Richard Bramble was born in London. He attended Sherborne School with an art scholarship, and graduated from the Slade School of Fine Art in 1990. Since then, his work has appeared in numerous exhibitions and collections around the country, including a selection for the Royal Academy Summer Exhibition. He continues to divide his time between London, Dorset and the Outer Hebrides.

The artist, as well as pursuing his landscape painting, continues to work with chefs painting kitchen scenes, food and ingredients. This has lead to a variety of commissions from wine producers to farmers.

As a development from the ingredient pages within the book, Richard has created a range of ingredient study prints, collections of which now adorn private kitchens as well as restaurants. Images range from well know ingredients such as coffee, chocolate and vanilla to more obscure subjects such as monkfish and rare breeds of cows.

In 2001, following his experience of working with the chefs and the ingredient studies, Jersey Pottery commissioned the artist to create a large range of ingredient, fish and shellfish plates made from limoge porcelain, in addition to place and serving mats.

To view and order the extensive range of pictures and plates, or enquire about commissions please go to the artist's website: www.richardbramble.co.uk
email: info@richardbramble.co.uk
Telephone: 020 7587 1471.

bibliography

The publishers are grateful to the following for permission to reprint certain recipes as listed:

Mussel Soup with Saffron
Sorbets with Lime Syrup
Rum Babas

taken from *Nico* by Nico Ladenis,
published by Pan Macmillan

Chicken with Vin Jaune

taken from *My Gastronomy*
by Nico Ladenis, published
by Pan Macmillan

Canapés with Sushi
Zucchini with Saffron Risotto
Loin of Lamb with a Mustard
and Herb Crust
Symphony of Fruit Purées

taken from *The Essential Mosimann*
by Anton Mosimann,
published by Ebury Press

Fishcakes with Parsley Sauce
Bread and Butter Pudding

taken from *Mosimann's World*
by Anton Mosimann,
published by Boxtree

Feuillantine of Raspberries
Roast Saddle of Rabbit

taken from *Wild Food From Land and Sea*
by Marco Pierre White,
published by Ebury Press

Grilled Squid with Chillies
Marinated Grilled Lamb
Lemon Tart
Chocolate Nemesis

taken from *The River Cafe Cook Book*
by Rose Gray and Ruth Rogers,
published by Ebury Press

Wood-Roasted Turbot Tranche
with Capers
Baked Fresh Borlotti Beans

taken from *The River Cafe Cook Book Two*
by Rose Gray and Ruth Rogers,
published by Ebury Press

Ravioli of Lobster
Tatin of Pears
Terrine of Pink Grapefruit,
Orange and Passion Fruit

taken from *Gordon Ramsay's*
Passion for Flavour
by Gordon Ramsay,
published by Conran Octopus

Larmes de Chocolat, Mousse
Ivoirine et Griottines

taken from *Desserts: A Lifelong Passion*
by Michel Roux,
published by Conran Octopus

Stuffed Pigs' Trotters with Morels
Salmon Cooked in Goose Fat
Pistachio Soufflé

taken from *Memories of Gascony*
by Pierre Koffmann,
published by Mitchell Beazley

Scallops with Squid Ink, Red
Pepper and Garlic Sauces

taken from *La Tante Claire*
by Pierre Koffmann,
published by Headline

Tagliatelle of Oysters
Lobster with its own Vinaigrette

taken from *White Heat*
by Marco Pierre White,
published by Mitchell Beazley

BIBLIOGRAPHY

Ackerman, R (ed) *The Chefs Compendium*, Alfresco.
Chapman, K *Great British Chefs 2*, Mitchell Beazley, London, 1995.
Dowell & Bailey, P & A *The Book of Ingredients*, Dorling Kindersley, 1980.
Duff, G *A Book of Herb and Spices*, Merchant Press, London, 1987.
Hopkinson, S *Roast Chicken and Other Stories*, Ebury, London, 1994.
Johnson, H *Hugh Johnson's Wine Companion*, Reed, London, 1997.
Morris, S *The New Guide to Spices Hermes House*, London, 1835.
Norwak, M *The Good Cook*, The Apple Press, 1985.
Roux, A & M *New Classic Cuisine*, Macdonald & Co, London, 1983.
Roux, M *Sauces*, Quadrille, 1996.
Stobart, T *The Cook's Encyclopaedia*, Cameron & Tayleur, 1980.

TOM AIKENS
www.tomaikens.co.uk
Tom Aikens
43 Elystan Street
London, SW3

RAYMOND BLANC
www.petit-blanc.com
Le Manoir aux Quat' Saisons
Church Roan, Great Milton, OX44 7PD
Tel. 01844 278 881

Le Petit Blanc
9 Brindley Place, Birmingham
Tel. 0121 633 7333

The Queen's Hotel,
The Promenade, Cheltenham
GL50 1NN
Tel. 01242 266 800

5 King Street,
Manchester M2 4LQ
Tel. 0161 832 1000

71-72 Walton Street,
Oxford OX2 6AG
Tel. 01865 510 999

MARTIN BLUNOS
Blinis
www.blinisbath.co.uk
16 Argyle Street, Bath BA2 4BQ
Tel. 01225 422 510

Martin Blunos at Fitzroys Brasserie
www.dukesbath.co.uk
Dukes Hotel, Greater Pulteney Street
Bath BA2 4DN
Tel. 01225 787 960

JOHN BURTON-RACE
www.landmarklondon.co.uk
John Burton-Race at The Landmark
222 Marylebone Road, London NW1
Tel. 020 7723 7800

MICHAEL CAINES
www.michaelcaines.com
Gidleigh Park
Chagford, Devon TQ13 8HH
Tel. 01647 432 225
www.gidleigh.com

Michael Caines at
The Royal Clarence
Cathedral Yard, Exeter EX1 1HD
Tel. 01392 310 031

ROSE GRAY AND RUTH ROGERS
www.rivercafe.co.uk
The River Café
Thames Wharf, Rainville Road,
London W6
Tel. 020 7386 4200

PAUL HEATHCOTE
www.simplyheathcotes.co.uk
Heathcote's Restaurant at Racasse
Canal Wharf, Leeds LS11 5PS
Tel. 01132 446 611

Paul Heathcote's Restaurant
104-106 Higher Road, Longridge
Preston PR3 3SY
Tel. 01772 784 969

Simply Heathcote's
25 The Strand,
Beetham Plaza, Liverpool L2 0XL
Tel. 0151 236 3536

Jackson's Row,
Manchester M2 4WD
Tel. 0161 835 3536

23 Winckley Square,
Preston PR1 3JJ
Tel. 01772 252 732

PHILIP HOWARD
www.squarerestaurant.com
The Square
6 Bruton Street, London, W1
Tel. 020 7495 7100

PIERRE KOFFMANN
www.savoy-group.co.uk
La Tante Claire
The Berkeley Hotel, Wilton Place,
London, W1
Tel. 020 7823 2003

NICO LADENIS
Deca
23 Conduit Street, London W1
Tel. 020 7493 7070

Incognico
117 Shaftesbury Avenue, London WC2
Tel. 020 7836 8866

ANTON MOSIMANN
www.mosimann.com
Mosimann's
11b West Halkin Street, London SW1
Tel. 020 7235 9625

ALAN MURCHINSON
www.ortolan.com
L'Ortolan
The Old Vicarge, Church Lane,
Shinfield, Berks RG2 9BY
Tel. 01189 883 783

JEAN-CHRISTOPHE NOVELLI
www.jeanchristophenovelli.com
Maison Novelli
29 Clerkenwell Green, London EC1
Tel. 020 7251 6606

SHANE OSBORN
www.pied.a.terre.co.uk
Pied a Terre
34 Charlotte Street, London, W1
Tel. 020 7636 1178

AARON PATTERSON
www.hambletonhall.co.uk
Hambleton Hall
Hambleton, Nr Oakham, Rutland
LE15 8TH
Tel. 01572 756 991

GORDON RAMSAY
www.gordonramsay.com
Gordon Ramsay
68 Royal Hospital Road, London SW3
Tel. 020 7352 4441

Gordon Ramsay at Claridge's
55 Brook Street, London, W1
Tel. 020 7499 0099

PAUL RANKIN
www.cayennerestaurant.com
Cayenne
7 Ascot House, Shaftsbury Square,
Belfast BT1 5EA
Tel. 01232 331 532

Café Paul Rankin
27-29 Fountain Street, Belfast
BT1 5EA
Tel. 01232 315 090

PAUL RHODES
www.paulandk.com
Paul & K
(Cookery courses/specialized catering)
31 Plough Way, London SE16
Tel. 020 7237 0837

MICHEL ROUX
www.waterside-inn.co.uk
The Waterside Inn
Ferry Road, Bray, Berkshire SL6 2AT
Tel. 01628 620 691

MICHEL ROUX JNR
www.le-gavroche.co.uk
Le Gavroche
43 Upper Brook Street, London W1
Tel. 020 7408 0881

MARCUS WAREING
www.gordonramsay.com
Pétrus
33 St James's Street, London SW1
Tel. 020 7930 4272

MARCO PIERRE WHITE
www.whitestarline.org.uk
Criterion
224 Piccadilly, London W1
Tel. 020 7930 0488

L'escargot
48 Greek Street, London W1
Tel. 020 7437 6828

Mirabelle
56 Curzon Street, London W1
Tel. 020 7499 4636

Quo Vadis
26-29 Dean Street, London W1
Tel. 020 7734 7333

index of recipes